WHAT A STATE!

BOLTONOMICS & THE APPALLING STATE OF BRITISH POLITICS

HENRY BOLTON OBE

WISE WALRUS

Published in the United Kingdom by:
Wise Walrus
3 Providence Cottages
White Horse Hill
Hawkinge
Kent, CT18 7AL

A CIP record of this book is available from the British Library.
First printed September 2019.

ISBN: 978-1-9162305-0-7

CONTENTS

PREFACE

HENRY BOLTON'S LITTLE BOOK OF BOLTONOMICS

By Lembit Öpik

Henry Bolton and I agree on a number of things. These include how to get to Central London from Tunbridge Wells, the time and the weather. But when it comes to agreeing about British politics... not so much. We've never campaigned for – or for that matter, against – each other. And we've never shared a desire to build a political party together. For me, it's the differences that make his book required reading.

To read the perspective of a senior figure in British politics at such a volatile time has given me the chance to test my own perspective versus that of another person who's thought extensively. His first hand experience of central matters facing the United Kingdom right now gives his assessment a vitality that reflects his emphatic and passionate personality.

This work isn't just about Brexit. Henry has highlighted areas that should be on the table for consideration at a strategic level. For example, has the 'liberal elite' created a new kind of intolerance - through the doubly ironic attempt to force worship at the alter of tolerance, while at the same time condemning those who don't conform to mainstream middle class views of society or the environment? He also asks: where's the leadership in British politics these days? How did Westminster find itself paralysed by the Brexit issue to the extent that – at the time I write this – it's already cost a couple of Prime Ministers their jobs? And why have so many 'experts' persistently mis-predicted the course of our economy?

I'm an outright libertarian. I truly believe humans are best served by personal liberty, with the state being responsible for creating a 'backstop' – if I may try to reclaim that word – to protect us from health, social and other hardships. To this extent, I'm something of an absolutist in a world of compromise: the world is not nearly as 'free' as I'd like it to be. Yet I found myself considering Henry Bolton's critical words on libertarianism as a counterpoint that can't be ignored. For instance, could it be that liberty is only effective when people don't misinterpret or discount the huge level of responsibility that comes with self-determination?

And what of the other inconvenient truths he seeks to highlight? Who really runs the country – 'incompetent negotiators' or 'unaccountable mandarins?' Has 'identity politics' undermined a more steady political ethos? And what of the emergence of new parties in response to an apparent public despair concerning the traditional two big hitters – Labour and Conservative?

I have my own views on a lot of these issues. Henry and I have argued them out many times, often without consensus. This process has caused me to recognise that there is always more to learn – that wisdom can't be downloaded or fast-tracked. It takes time and experience and, crucially, the skill of listening without prejudice to those with something meaningful to say. Henry is one of those people. As he reminds us, George Bernard Shaw famously stated: 'those who cannot change their minds cannot change anything.' It seems necessary, therefore, to know the alternatives to one's own position, because you can't change your mind if you don't know you need to.

Essentially, Henry Bolton's motivation is to get us all to think through the realities in a British political epoch unlike any which has gone before. He's been a central figure on the frontline in a battle involving a political spectrum that has been instrumental in getting the country to where it found itself. He's therefore rather well placed to suggest what should happen next.

This 'little book' as he calls it, can have big consequences at a time when expedience has often appeared to strangle principle. Say what you like about Brexit, Henry's political positioning and his ambition to provide a solid alternative to the movements he feels have had their day. His candid analysis adds great value and I salute him for it. I believe it provides a glimpse of the unresolved disputes to come. At a time when the political community seems wedded to offering 'bolt on' solutions as quick fixes to massive structural problems, Henry's more profound approach feels a great deal more thought out.

So, start reading this positive alternative to the poorly fashioned party agendas which currently blight Britain. Underline the bits you like, highlight the bits you don't, and finish up wiser than when you started. That's what Henry Bolton is dedicated to achieving with his 'little book' on

British politics and economics. And, as far as I'm concerned, he succeeds.

Lembit Öpik

British Member of Parliament for Montgomeryshire, 1997-2010

Shadow Secretary of State for Northern Ireland, 1998-2008

Leader of the Welsh Liberal Democrats, 2001-2007

AUTHOR'S NOTE

Throughout this book, I have made observations and drawn conclusions that I believe to be correct. They are, of course, based on the information I have. If that information is incorrect then my conclusions may also be. Furthermore, it is difficult to predict the future with absolute certainty. That said if, despite my best efforts to avoid it, this book contains any errors of fact or analysis, I apologise in advance.

At a time of great moment; at the dawn of inevitable change, there is perhaps little that is more important than objective thinking, vision, leadership and an imaginative approach to the challenges we all face. It is for that reason, without apology, that I refer frequently in this book to the context of Brexit and the United Kingdom's departure from the European Union.

How we perceive the challenges we face, indeed whether we identify and acknowledge them at all and, if we do, how we address them, will shape our nation, the inhabitants of these islands and the attitudes of our friends and allies abroad for decades to come.

The responsibility placed upon the politicians of today, concerning the people of the UK tomorrow, is therefore immense. I fear they are not up to the task.

Many of the subjects I have touched upon are sensitive and contentious. I have no doubt whatsoever that I shall receive praise for this book, but I will also receive huge hostility and criticism. That is the unfortunate reality of modern politics.

However, my intention is to contribute constructively to everyone's thinking on what is happening to our nation, why and what might be done about it. And, at this point, it is worth pointing out that I use the term 'nation' to encompass all of the people with the right to call the United Kingdom of Great Britain and Northern Ireland, home.

My aim, above all, is to provoke thought; to remove the blinkers of conventional or mainstream thinking and to trigger some degree of broader and perhaps more strategic consideration of the issues facing politicians and society today. To that end, the reader will observe that I have not only addressed the more obvious issues of the day, such as the UK's departure from the EU, but that I have also addressed some sensitive subjects, for example, terrorism and the sentence of death for treason, equal representation versus equal opportunities and the perversion of our national history. I have also employed some contentious examples, such as Britains role in the global abolition of slavery, so as to provoke reaction and therefore consideration of certain issues.

I have been forthright in expressing my views on the quality of our politicians. I have not done so to offend and hope I have not done so. Rather my purpose in this regard is clear communication. I hope that my comments, even should you disagree with them, will be taken by readers as critically constructive in their intent, even if they are contentious.

I have attempted to make my little book easy to read, albeit I have been challenged by the fact that politics, economics and related issues can be immensely tedious and dry.

I have found myself experiencing varying degrees of emotion, passion and frustration when writing. I suspect this comes across to the reader. At first, I attempted to suppress it and not allow those feelings to be communicated in these pages, but then I reflected that it may not be such a bad thing if to some degree the passion and conviction I feel comes across. I have tried not to rant. No doubt you will judge whether or not I've got the balance right.

If all you do, is dip into this book now and again, I will be happy. If you react to what you read, if it makes you curious or triggers any thoughts, irritation, satisfaction or pleasure, or perhaps even a wry smile or two, I will have achieved a part of my aim of provoking reflection.

Lembit Opik, my friend and oft political sparring partner - an activity that involves numerous glasses "of the red" - has termed my insistence on justifying all political decisions against their contribution towards the confidence, optimism, prosperity and security of the nation as 'Boltonomics'. If you adopt that term, or simply buy into my argument that we must lift our eyes towards the future and national aspiration, I shall be immensely pleased. That in itself will encourage some degree of change for the better.

Finally, let me leave you with this thought:

We cannot solve our problems with the same thinking we used when we created them.

Albert Einstein

Thank you for buying this little book. I sincerely hope you find it interesting and enjoy it.

Henry Bolton
Folkestone
August 2019

SOME WISE WORDS TO START

"All men make mistakes, but a good man yields when he knows his course is wrong and repairs the evil. The only crime is pride."

Sophocles, Antigone

"When you come out of the storm, you won't be the same person who walked in. That's what this storm's all about."

Haruki Murakami, Kafka on the Shore

Breathes there the man with soul so dead,
Who never to himself hath said,
This is my own, my native land!
Whose heart hath ne'er within him burn'd,

As home his footsteps he hath turn'd
From wandering on a foreign strand!
If such there breathe, go, mark him well;

For him no Minstrel raptures swell;
High though his titles, proud his name,
Boundless his wealth as wish can claim;
Despite those titles, power, and pelf,
The wretch, concentred all in self,
Living, shall forfeit fair renown,
And, doubly dying, shall go down
To the vile dust, from whence he sprung,
Unwept, unhonour'd, and unsung.

Sir Walter Scott

"It is not the critic who counts; not the man who points out how the strong man stumbles, or where the doer of deeds could have done them better. The credit belongs to the man who is actually in the arena, whose face is marred by dust and sweat and blood; who strives valiantly; who errs, who comes short again and again, because there is no effort without error and shortcoming; but who does actually strive to do the deeds; who knows great enthusiasms, the great devotions; who spends himself in a worthy cause; who at the best knows in the end the triumph of high achievement, and who at the worst, if he fails, at least fails while daring greatly, so that his place shall never be with those cold and timid souls who neither know victory nor defeat."

President Theodore Roosevelt

"Those who cannot change their minds cannot change anything."

George Bernard Shaw

"We know what we are, but not what we may be."

William Shakespeare

PROLOGUE

"WHEN YOU COME OUT OF THE STORM, YOU WON'T BE THE SAME PERSON WHO WALKED IN. THAT'S WHAT THIS STORM'S ALL ABOUT." - HARUKI MURAKAMI

The entire Brexit debacle has fundamentally undermined already weak public trust in our politics and our politicians. It is quite possible that, by the time you read this book, the United Kingdom will have left the European Union. However, it will take many years, even with fair winds and a following sea, to undo the damage to public confidence done by Theresa May's prevarication and the subsequent political games played out between Leave and Remain MPs in parliament.

Those games have not only been played out between Leave and Remain supporters, but also between those who believe in the deep resilience of our institutions and the strengths of our constitution on the one hand, and those who seek to use the Brexit debate as a way of achieving constitutional reform on the other. The later group seek exploit the Brexit debate to obtain a codified, socialist constitution, that would wrest significant executive authority from the government and place it in the hands of the House of Commons, through the back door. The relevance of the Monarch would be seriously weakened and the relationship and balance of power between the legislative and the executive fundamentally disturbed.

There are then the significant challenges facing the UK outside the EU. The most fundamental of these are not related to our membership, or otherwise, of the Brussels block. They are internal. They lie, and will continue to lie, within our own society, legislation, institutions, media and politics. Whether we, as a nation, are able and willing to recognise those challenges, whether we are serious in wanting to address them and if so how we do, will have a much greater bearing on the confidence, prosperity and stability of our country than any trade deal, greater indeed than any agreements we may reach on the global stage. These internal challenges and how we approach them are what this book is about.

History will make its own judgement of the present turmoil and character of British politics. Although we might guess what that judgement will be, how future generations will actually interpret this period, who they will see as the villains and who as the good guys, it is impossible to predict. But judge they will, and it will be through the social, ethical and political lens of their time, not of ours. How they judge will, in large part no doubt, be based upon what they think the impact of our decisions (in their past) will have had on their lives (in our future).

This book is an attempt therefore to raise the eyes of its readers to the future and to the issues we must address now if that future is to be a bright and positive one.

We are in a storm. When we come out of it we will not be the same nation, the same people, that entered it. That, as Haruki Murakami wrote, is what this storm is all about. It is about change. But to manage and cope with change we must have a vision to lead and guide us, to steer us through and beyond the storm and into the future.

My vision is of a confident, optimistic, prosperous, secure and globally outward looking trading nation, respected by our friends, allies and enemies alike.

That is my vision. That is my aspiration and aim for this great country of ours as we walk out of the storm and into our future and I commend it to you all.

Our task now must be to set the conditions for achieving that vision and to get on with the work of making it a reality. All efforts and all policies myst be orientated towards that aim.

1

THE TRIGGER - WHAT BROUGHT THIS BOOK ABOUT

There are many things about present day British politics that should be of grave concern to us all. However, in a typically British way, we've deferred to our political elite in Westminster, presuming that they do, ultimately, know best.

We have just gone along with things in a way that perhaps the peoples of other countries and cultures would not have done. We may grumble in the pubs and when we meet each other in the street, but we, or very few of us, become truly militant as perhaps the French, Italians and other more passionate peoples may do.

Yet, we all see the erosion of society, of moral and social values, community, pride, public services and even, hope, all across our islands.

Now though, something has brought us close to the brink. Something has exposed the incompetence, negligence and self-serving arrogance of Westminster MPs and many of the most senior Whitehall civil servants for what it is; we finally realise that those who occupy the highest offices in the land and those who advise them, do not always know best and are not necessarily working with the interests of others foremost in their minds. Something has just about brought the people of our islands to cry "Enough!".

That thing is the appalling, ubelievable, negligent, mendacious and astoundingly incompetent handling of the entire Brexit process.

In the build-up to the 23rd June 2016 referendum, I was working in Brussels as an EU Common Security and Defence Policy (CSDP) Planner. This was a relatively senior position, I led the EU planning team in Ukraine during the crisis in 2014 and subsequently, briefly, Headed of the EU Advisory Mission in Ukraine, normally an ambassadorial post. I also held the portfolio for civilian CSDP border management planning outside the EU. I frequently held discussions with national EU member state ambassadors and the with most senior officials in the European Commission. I can say with authority, the general feeling in Brussels and member state capitals during the build up to the referendum was that the Brits would vote to remain in the EU.

However, there was also serious concern that, in the unlikely event that the UK indeed voted to 'Leave', British negotiators would run rings around their Brussels counterparts.

The chairman of one of the ambassadorial committees that prepares EU heads of government meetings said to me, "You Brits don't say very much, but when you do, it's always from a position of knowledge, after careful consideration and with sound common sense. Everything you say is pertinent and even if we don't agree, we always take note of what you say. We would be lunatics not to. You [Brits] are the best in the business and, yes, we are worried that if you leave, you are going dominate negotiations entirely".

Of course we did vote, by a majority of over one and a quarter million, to leave. Then, Theresa May, her chief negotiator, Ollie Robins, the Chancellor, Philip Hammond, the cabinet as a whole and the senior civil service, as an institutional group, all subsequently let the country down to an incredible, inexcusable and unforgivable degree that will take us years to recover from.

Our reputation as an effective and influential player on the European and global stage has taken a massive hit, not by our vote to leave, but by the May government's appallingly naive approach to the negotiations and by the behaviour of our parliamentarians.

Nearly two years later, in 2018 I met the same person for a coffee at St Pancras Station, in London. He was incredulous.

"We thought you'd come to the table with a watertight set of objectives, demands and a full plan. You didn't. You came and asked what we wanted. We were astounded. How could we answer that? You are the ones leaving. We couldn't believe it and started to wonder what game London was playing. We were thinking, well, clearly they [May's government] have a plan, so why are they giving us the impression they haven't? What are they up to? They must have something up their sleeve.' But then we gradually began to realise that you actually didn't; that there was, and still is, no plan. It was obvious that Mrs May wanted to deliver Brexit but also to stay joined at the hip to us. I can't describe the amazement. I think we still don't really believe it." he continued.

"I'm sorry to say that your Prime Minister and government have let you down. We really didn't think we'd be able to match you, but Mrs May still doesn't have a clue and the cabinet has no idea how the EU works, even now. How can that be? How can your once great country have allowed itself to get into this situation?

I have repeatedly asked myself the same question. This book reflects some of my thoughts about that and tries to address some of the reasons as to why we're in this situation and I make some suggestions what might be done about it.

2

THE STATE OF POLITICS

There is no doubting that British politics are in an almighty mess, but why?

There are several reasons, all of which I explore in detail in later chapters. For the moment though, it is worth touching on them in general:

Brexiteers, whilst focusing heavily on achieving and winning the referendum in 2016, failed to provide a national vision and plan for what would happen afterwards and stopped campaigning when the vote was won. They gave up the initiative and momentum that they had worked so hard to gain and there was no resistance when, as was I had predicted, the Remain camp re-organised and came back with a vengeance. There was a negligent and naive assumption on the part of Brexiteer leaders that, if we won the referendum, our departure from the EU was a given. Winning the referendum was considered as 'job done'. I argued passionately at the time that it wasn't the case, that the real work had to start at that point because winning the referendum was about being able to deliver something tangible for the British people. But my concerns fell on the deaf ears of populistic celebration and fervour. The ball was dropped, allowing room for uncertainty and other agendas to establish themselves and grow. These agendas factionalised and weakened Leave organisations and gave space for Remain campaigners to mobilise in an attempt to stop Brexit.

A classic example was UKIP. Nigel Farage resigned the leadership immediately after the referendum. Subsequent leadership failed to replace the unifying purpose of winning the referendum, allowing divergent politics to play out within the Party. By the time I took over the leadership in September 2017, it had broken into factions. My efforts to herd the cats, halt and reverse the party's slide towards the right and to reform the party into a cohesive, constructive contributor to the national Brexit debate were opposed and thwarted at every turn by a National Executive Committee many members of which were affiliated to various factions. In their opposition to me the NEC was aided by a couple of MEPs: Bill Etheridge and Gerard Batten, and two allies of the NEC, Ben Walker and Annabelle Fuller. The political intellect of these people was simply incapable of grasping anything more complex than protest politics. The lunatics had taken over the asylum and it was beyond rescue. They have reaped their reward. The Brexit Party has stepped in to take UKIPs place and, at the time of writing, in the run up to the 2019 General Election, the Party is polling at less than 1%. The disruption to the Brexit message and cause was not insignificant.

Similar fictionalisation, driven by simplistic, self-interested, opportunistic, personal ambition and agenda, characterises much of British politics and is being played out in other parties and in the Palace of Westminster. It is symptomatic of a lack of intellect and altruistic leadership across the political class.

Another reason for the mess that is British politics is that for decades a large proportion of our national assembly – Parliament: both Commons and Lords – has been comprised of characterless, unqualified political equivocators who cannot think outside the box and have no imagination; people whose first loyalty is to themselves and their ego and their second to their party. Most lack any sort of leadership ability and possess little or no concept of the traits of leadership as different from management. The presence of such a large number of such people has altered the nature and character of the Commons and of our government.

Additionally, our Whitehall civil service is institutionally orientated towards the European Union.

Then there is the widespread acceptance in politics and activism of the terms "progressive society", "progressive politics" and of the growth of "identity politics". This has led to greater moral and social self-indulgence and a decline generally.

Furthermore, three other influences have combined to undermine the quality and of our national politicians:

- The concentration of politics around the centre ground;
- Tribal voting;
- The governance framework and decision making procedures of the European Union and their impact on our government and the civil service.

All these issues and more are discussed in the following pages.

3

HISTORY, THE ATTEMPT TO PERVERT OUR NATIONAL IDENTITY AND THE DEGRADATION OF OUR POLITICAL SOCIETY

"PEOPLE WHO TAKE NO PRIDE IN THE NOBLE ACHIEVEMENTS OF REMOTE ANCESTORS WILL NEVER ACHIEVE ANYTHING WORTHY TO BE REMEMBERED WITH PRIDE BY REMOTE DESCENDANTS." - THOMAS MACAULAY

As a nation and as individuals our character, perceptions and values are created and shaped by our history. On the pother hand the future is crafted by us and is in our own hands. In this respect, we would do well to understand and learn from the experiences of the past, not only from those that support our own objectives and reinforce our own world view.

People make judgements about the past. That is natural and inevitable. History exists and our interest in it is born out of a human desire to understand who we are and to learn. It is equally natural to make judgements based upon the instinctive habit of comparing ourselves with others and the present with the past.

It is equally inevitable that judgements will be made of the decisions made by people in past ages. Interestingly though, our critical judgements appear to apply almost exclusively to the more recent European past, going back to the Industrial and French revolutions and, to an extent, the dawn of European colonialism in the 1500's, but no further.

Those judgements are frequently emotive and focus on the authorities, institutions, politicians and characters of Europe and the United States over the last 500 years or so. Interestingly, they are not applied to regimes and rulers before then.

Few positive judgements are made regarding history. They tend to be critical. How often, for example, have you heard someone point to a really good historical example as a guide to what we should do in the present? There are, however, many critical and condemnatory judgements that are selectively chosen and applied to support the anti-establishment political causes of the today.

That said, we hear few condemnatory judgements of the Roman Empire, early (pre-historical) slavery, the behaviour of the Golden Hoards of Ghengis Khan as they swept across Central Asia, or the atrocities committed by the Turks and the Christian Crusaders. Why is that? Why does the condemnation of history and historical characters only seem to apply to the last 500 years or so?

I believe it is because, to be useful in getting a point across, history must be relevant to the present. Therefore the examples most often sought or referred to in the UK are linked in some way to European culture, society, politics and the modern era - modern in this case meaning post the dawn of the industrial revolution.

If comparisons between the past and the present are approached from a contextual and objective point of view, it is for the good. If approached out of context, and presented selectively, with the purpose of furthering a political cause or belief, comparisons can be damaging and dangerous. In tailoring or interpreting history to suit our present day agendas we are manipulating opinions for our own ends and laying the seeds for disagreement, division, prejudice and certainly political discord and conflict.

If we make judgements of who did what in history, why and how, and of what was good and what not, those judgements will, of course, be made within the frame of what we have been told of history and how it was presented to us.

Those judgements of the past, in turn, because they are lessons, shape our behaviour, now, in the present.

So, it is important that our judgements are well informed and sound. Our knowledge of history must be comprehensive, complete and objective rather than subjective.

Yet, the history taught in schools today is generally incomplete and often presented in subjective manner. History teachers and lecturers often express their own interpretation and political perspectives when describing historical events. This, in my view, is an unforgivable abuse of their position and a manipulation of the perceptions of their students.

We must remove the subjective judgement of history in education. We must ensure that it is comprehensive, complete and within the context of the time and social, political and economic environment. We must bring back an appreciation of the importance of context and objectivity in education. Teachers must teach students how to analyse what they learn, and not tell them or imply what the result of that analysis should be.

The value of studying history is in learning its lessons; in helping us to better manage the present and the future and in building an understanding of who we are; to satisfy the human need for of identity.

However, as I said earlier, we are seeing a powerful tendency towards criticism of the past motivated, consciously or otherwise, by the agendas of today. It is common that historical lessons are selected and presented to students in a way that reinforces a political message. This invariably means those lessons are used critically. It is not for teachers to do that. Teachers must impart knowledge and analysis, not pursue political causes. It is for students then to use that knowledge to help them to draw their own conclusions in relation to the present day. Yet, too frequently, history is being re-shaped to suit today's political agendas.

There are plenty of lessons to teach us that the selective application of history is incredibly dangerous.

The Nazi regime of Germany, the authorities of the Soviet Union, Enver Hoxha's dictatorship in Albania and many others, sought to do the same; to re-write history, be selective about or leave out 'lessons' that contradicted the policies of the governing party. The aim was always to alter the historical emphasis of past events and shape perceptions so as to reinforce the politics and policies of the party, cause or regime.

Interestingly, in the modern era, most such authoritarian governments have grown out of communism or deeply socialist, left-wing politics.

The original name of National Socialist Party (NAZI Party) of Germany was 'National Socialist German Workers' Party. That may provide a clue as to its origin and doctrine.

Enver Hoxha was the First Secretary of the Labour Party of Albania

Re-shaping history, or applying it in support of, or to justify political causes, is unacceptable. It falsifies identity, builds and sustains support for authoritarian regimes and leads to social suppression of challenges to the established order or to a particular set of political views or agendas.

Indeed, I would argue that the focus on criticising characters and events in British history, on focusing on the negative and disregarding the positive chapters of our national story, has contributed to the sense that there is nothing to be proud of in being British. This has in turn made it politically sensitive to talk about being British. We are supposed to be embarrassed by our Britishness. Our national identity has thereby been weakened. But human beings are intrinsically social animals. We have and instinctive need to belong to a group. But if we can't be British, then what other group can we belong to? LGBTQ? BME? Muslim? Christian? Remainers? Leavers? The EU?

The unbalanced and critical way that we have taught recent generations to view the history of the British people has contributed significantly to the fragmentation of society.

Furthermore, I believe this is, if not deliberate, the result of political partisanship and bias on the part of the educationalists involved.

Politicians and their supporters throughout the centuries have perverted history for their own purposes, however, I fear that extremists on the left, right and indeed also the centre of British politics are themselves doing exactly this and have been for some time. Good people must resist this phenomenon and students should question the motives, integrity and ethics of any teacher or lecturer who is interpreting and drawing conclusions on their behalf.

History is, of course, full of the bad actions, as well as the good, of extraordinary men and woman. All the most noted people have done both good things and bad. However, the focus is invariably on the bad. Campaigners have called for statues of Cecil Rhodes, Clive of India and Churchill to be removed, forgetting - or perhaps choosing to forget - that, had it not been for the good practices, ideas, ambitions and achievements of occasionally flawed, often dislikable and frequently difficult personalities of the past, we would not now benefit from the social values, laws, justice, prosperity and civilisation of the present.

Of course, such things as slavery must be condemned without compromise. It is a heinous and unforgivable crime that can never be tolerated. However, we must remember, without in any way justifying it, that slavery was, for many millennia, the norm, worldwide. We know it existed 4,500 years ago and quite probably many thousands of years before that. The people who in 2006 called on Tony Blair to apologise for the UK's involvement in slavery, 200 years after its abolition, were enthusiastically critical of their (our) country, its history and its involvement in slavery, but denied many historical facts and refused entirely to give some credit where it is due. Their's was and is an unbalanced, critical, judgemental and political motivated position. It was not an objective position based on a comprehensive knowledge and understanding of history.

These campaigners re-shaped history to suit their ends. They happily ignored the fact that it was the anti-slavery campaign in Great Britain, yes, Great Britain, that provided the impetus and momentum that in turn led to the global abolition of the trade in human beings; that ended many thousands of years of the despicable practice. They utterly failed, perhaps deliberately so, to recognise that had it not been for our influence across the globe, our Empire and power, we could not have had such a significant and beneficial impact.

True, whilst slavery is now illegal everywhere, it is still prolific as a criminal practice in some places. So, there is still much work to be done. However, the fact is that many people simply cannot abide the idea that our great nation has been a massive influence for good in the world; that, historically, we have at least as much to be proud of as ashamed of.

There are too many people who, out of habit or perhaps even fashion, love to talk our country down rather than up. These are the same people who will, undoubtedly, condemn the comments I make in this book. They learn and apply history's negative lessons, but often fail to acknowledge the positive ones or that there is both good and bad in most things. Perhaps this is why society is so critical of everything and everyone these days. Everything is seen in a bad light and very little as positive, good and worthy of praise. This is important so, indulge me whilst I provide some facts, using slavery as an example.

Concerted moves to end slavery started in the UK.

After a slow start in 1787, a Bill applying the abolition of the slave trade to all British territories globally was passed in both Houses of the UK Parliament in 1807. This Bill was superseded by the Abolition of Slavery Act in 1833 which outlawed the slave trade altogether. It was a massive step forward and triggered policies that led to the eventual abolition of slavery around the world, including in the United States.

In the space of some 46 years, between 1787 and 1833, Great Britain overturned an appalling abuse that had, until then, been globally prolific for many thousands of years. We outlawed the slave trade not only at home but also throughout our colonial possessions abroad. Quite an achievement.

Why was it us British, not some other nation, that finally turned against slavery and was able to achieve its legal abolition world wide?

One reason is that we are, as a nation, generally and by tradition and custom, profoundly compassionate and nonconformist. Another is that we were the World's leading superpower, possessed of an Empire and therefore of the influence and reach needed to make a significant global impact. A third and hugely important factor was that we had leaders prepared to challenge the status quo and, as a nation, we believed in ourselves and had confidence in our ability to deliver positive change.

Slavery is but one example. We Brits were also behind the creation of NATO, the United Nations and the establishment of human rights principles across the globe.

Given that background, and given the importance of our confidence and non-conformity as a nation - as a people - as a pre-requisit in achieving incredible and positive things, I now have cause to worry.

I worry that we are becoming, perhaps have become, politically conformist. For the first time in the history of our islands, campaigners, activists, the media and weak, characterless politicians have managed to smother the intrinsic characteristics and strengths of the British people.

The simple fact is that the British people have always provided the world with leadership. Slavery is largely a thing of the past, in large part due to the efforts of an earlier and far less altruistic generation of British campaigners and political leaders than we have now. But similarly, significant and crucial challenges face the modern world and must also be addressed. However, they also require real international leadership. Such challenges include environmental damage to our oceans, atmosphere, flora, fauna, water, agriculture and fisheries; overpopulation; massive rates of migration; the need to source sustainable energy.

Where is the vision, sagacity, strategic acumen, moral and physical courage and the leadership that the world needs to address these challenges?

Until recently, our society somehow always managed to learn, improve and apply common sense and enlightened values. This would not have been possible had it not been for the objective recognition that we had of our history, of who we are, warts and all. In recent years though, it has become politically incorrect to acknowledge the positive aspects of our past; anyone who sticks their head above the parapet to encourage confidence in being British and in our ability to lead, is likely to have it shot off by those who can't abide the idea that we Brits can stand proudly on our own two feet and actually do have something to offer the world.

Why is it that in the past we were able to find it in ourselves to address and resolve, at least in large part, the important issues not only of our islands, but of the world, but cannot do so now? Why is our modern society and political leadership failing us?

Well, I believe that some people deliberately and selectively reject or criticise our history and our identity, including those who influence the education and perceptions of new generations. I believe that they have embarked upon a conscious effort to dumb down the relevance of history and its lessons for identity, unity and both good and bad example; an effort to dumb down rather than develop individual excellence and character. I believe that this effort will, if left unchecked and if successful, destroy our ability, as the British people, to inspire and bring about positive change at home and abroad.

I will, no doubt, be criticised for harking back to past glories. None the less I shall do so now. Past generations would laud me for it; some members of the present generation will condemn me for it, but I'm unashamedly going to talk briefly of the British Empire.

The Empire is criticised through the prism of today's world and its improved knowledge and values. Yet, without the Empire and the relationship that the UK had with the peoples of India, Canada, Australia, New Zealand, East and South Africa and what is now the Commonwealth; without Britain's leadership and our historical links with the United States, it would have been impossible to mobilise the manpower and resources needed to successfully address slavery or defend the liberty of Europe from both Kaiser Wilhelm's Germany and Hitler's Third Reich. It would not have been possible to roll back the Japanese threat to the independence of the nations of the Far East or to stand against the Soviet Union in the Cold War. It was Winston Churchill who coined the phrase 'Iron Curtain' and mobilised the west to stand firm against Moscow's suppression of Eastern and Central Europe. Arguably, it was his foresight, courage, strategic acumen and leadership that put in place the policies and institutions that eventually led, many years after his death, to the eventual lifting of that Iron Curtain and the independence of West Germany and the Near Eastern countries of Europe. He recognised that the West had to play a long game. Which politician these days shows any ability or readiness to grasp the fact that some things just cannot be achieved in five years, or for that matter in a lifetime. Yet those things are still worth doing.

That all said, things change. The two world wars and their associated cost in human life and treasure encouraged and fuelled already embryonic independence movements and accelerated the call for self-government across the colonial world - a good thing. The days of the Empire were numbered and nothing demonstrated Britain's decline as a world power more clearly than the Suez Crisis of 1956.

None the less, today we still have every reason to be confident and to believe in ourselves.

The British economy is the fifth largest in the world; we are one of only five permanent members of the UN Security Council; we are the second most powerful NATO member state (second only to the United States), our native language is the language of international law, business, aviation and the seas and we lead the world in many areas of technology and engineering.

Yet, incredibly, many choose to deny not only our history but our extant skills, knowledge and entrepreneurship. They say: "but we are a small, insignificant country and cannot possibly survive outside the European Union".

I suggest that the real 'Little Englanders' are not those who want to take a place on the global stage, but are those who do not believe that we can make our way in the world; those who would have us step back from international leadership and example and who deny and even attempt to bury our intrinsic character and advantages as a nation. In doing so, they unquestionably harm our ability to support our citizens at home and to provide inspiration for others abroad.

Whilst I believe such people to be lacking in imagination, self-less ambition and intellect, I cannot blame them for questioning our national capacity. After all, since the Suez crisis, our politicians have utterly failed to provide any leadership for the British People, or any unifying vision for the future of our nation, towards which we can all aspire.

Increasingly, those of us who believe in Britain; who believe in the British people, our entrepreneurs, businesses, scientists, engineers, doctors, nurses, servicemen and women and who believe the UK can be an inspiration and beacon of hope for others, are abused, threatened and occasionally attacked on social media and in the streets by those who do not.

Political correctness has moved ridiculously far beyond the principles of fair play, common decency and good manners. Equal opportunities and social cohesion have been undermined by the emergence of identity politics and equal representation.

The majority of people are now fearful of expressing legitimate opinions and deterred from discussing reasonable concerns in public. They are rightfully worried they may be abused or labelled as in some way prejudiced, bigoted or simply stupid. 'Trolls', primarily, although not exclusively on the far left of the political spectrum, through online bullying work to close down the expression of political views other than their own on social media.

Intimidation, violence and the threat of violence against politicians of all parties, their families and friends, has become not only commonplace, but a feature of their everyday life.

Far ranging, permissive and damaging changes have been made to our institutions: the civil service, education, health-care, police, judicial system and the armed forces. Who are the anonymous figures none of us elected but who have introduced the so called 'progressive' changes that none of us voted for?

Violent crime is rising, prisons are likened to holiday camps with drugs being freely available to inmates, many of whom continue to run organised crime groups from within the walls. We spend more and more on healthcare, yet surgerics are closing and we remain well behind many other OECD nations in terms of patient diagnosis, care and outcomes in several areas.

We have allowed the native practices of some immigrant communities to continue here in the UK, thereby undoing many years of advances in equality and animal welfare. We never voted for these changes. They were never presented in any manifesto. Who has taken it upon themselves to introduce and allow these changes, and who has failed to stop them? Who can stop them?

Our politicians, particularly those in the Palace of Westminster, have humiliated the country over Brexit, and have repeatedly failed to act in the interests of the British People. The repeatedly make promises and break them. Too many politicians lack the life experience, intellectual tools, knowledge, courage and integrity to make appropriate decisions. This is a reflection of the politics of self-interest exercised by the political parties that select these people as candidates.

Our country's growth may be defined by a rise in wealth, or in our capacity to supply increasingly diverse economic goods. But it should also be defined by the happiness and emotional health and wellbeing of our population. These two things are different but are connected. To address both the measurable wealth and capacity of the economy and the happiness and contentment of the nation requires complex thinking and solutions and they must be addressed concurrently by the government at all levels. That demands intellect, imagination, strategic acumen, leadership and the ability to 'challenge whilst serving'. How many of our politicians have those attributes? Very few I would suggest.

We have a rich, vibrant history that we should, in many respects if not all, be immensely proud of. However, there is also much about Great Britain that must be mended if we are to become and feel a confident, optimistic, prosperous and secure as we emerge from the Brexit story and journey into the future.

Politicians must urgently raise their eyes to a national vision and the longer-term future, perhaps beyond their own careers or even lives, if they are to make the right decisions in the present. I fear, however, that none of the present generation of national politicians are up to the task.

The aim of this little book is to contribute towards the process of change, unity and the post-Brexit mending process by provoking thought and, hopefully, some degree of strategic insight and leadership, so that we can indeed become a more confident, optimistic, prosperous and secure, globally outward looking trading nation that is able to inspire and lead others as well as ourselves.

4

IMMIGRANTS & BORDERS

The short-sighted and naïve manner in which successive governments have managed immigration beggars belief and for many reasons we must discuss this sensitive and divisive subject.

Let me pose this question for you:

Is increasing the population by around 300,000 people every year, whilst cutting policing by 20%, and local government by some 50% as the Conservative government has done since 2011, sustainable?

Of course, it is not. Something must give. Something must change, and saying so is not racist or xenophobic. It is a matter of good governance. It is a matter of securing the welfare not only of the people already living in these islands, but also that of those who may attempt to reach the UK. It is a matter of the responsibility to manage immigration well.

In 2018, the population of the UK was 66,500,000. The Office for National Statistics estimates that by 2030 it will have increased by another 4,852,687 or 7.3% to 71,352,687, an average annual increase between now (2019) and then of 404,390.

Net immigration in 2017 (280,000) represented 70% of the annual population increase and equated to the population of Newcastle upon Tyne.

Undoubtedly, this places a massive demand on housing and public services and requires an enhancement of both. It is an inescapable fact that around half the demand for housing (and a proportionate pressure on the environment and the green belt) is due to immigration.

The Conservative governments under Prime Ministers Cameron and May slashed policing, local government and public service budgets. This has multiplied the destabilising impact of immigration and has fuelled community tensions and resentment, much of which has been turned on immigrant communities themselves rather than the politicians and faceless officials responsible for it.

The existential risk to the European way of life is not from immigration itself, but from the rate and scale of immigration; from the sheer number of people arriving from other cultures and, without judging them, with different social norms and habits to our own. The rate of immigration is also such that it is beyond the capacity of the government to manage it effectively.

Furthermore, communities are struggling to adjust. Immigrants lack the encouragement to assimilate into UK society and are often, worryingly, unwilling to do so.

The situation is an unholy mess. The government must be persuaded to reduce immigration and manage it a lot more thoughtfully and effectively if we are to avoid ever increasing social division and tension.

The persecution by what has been termed the liberal left

and social liberals, of anyone who hints at criticism of the government's appalling record on, and management of, immigration, is nothing short of a repressive contravention of the right to free speech and flies in the face of decent human behaviour.

Expressing concern at the rate of immigration, its impact on communities and arguing for more effort to be made to integrate immigrants into our society, does not equate in any way to being racist. To suggest it does, as some do, is inaccurate, ridiculous, and dangerous.

Who are these frequently anonymous abusers who attempt to suppress legitimate opinion? Who do they think they represent? What reasoned and persuasive argument are they prepared to present? None. They are divisive and obstruct the constructive thinking and debate that supports and develops thinking and solutions in a civilised, stable democratic society.

The government's negligence in managing immigration is doing significant social harm and if people or politicians sincerely believe that government policy is wrong, they must be free to say so without being subjected to a stream of abuse.

It is not only the inability of national and local infrastructure and services to cope with the rate of immigration that is of concern. Ensuring that communities are not forced to absorb change that undermines social confidence and optimism is vital. To neglect this is to accept community insecurity and social tension.

It is entirely natural for people to feel insecure when the environment they live in changes too rapidly, in ways and with implications they cannot predict. However, this is precisely what has been happening, particularly since the

1980s.

Too many communities have been subjected to a rate of change resulting from immigration that has left them feeling insecure and uncertain. They didn't vote for badly managed immigration, so who imposed it upon them?

I have to be very clear on a couple of points:

Firstly, this situation is not the fault of immigrants. Who can blame someone who sees the opportunity to better their lot and that of their family, and grasps that opportunity with both hands? The fault lies with our incompetent, weak politicians and faceless civil servants. Enough is enough. We must make these people accountable for their decisions.

If the nation truly wants to help economic migrants (see the next chapter for my views own that), we must stop simply opening our doors to them. We must instead generate an effective strategy for making staying in their own countries a far more attractive option.

And a simple, inescapable fact is that the majority of immigrants that travel across the EU to reach the Channel coast are not refugees. They are economic migrants. They may have originally left their country of origin as refugees, however they have since transited a number of safe countries before reaching the Channel coast.

Under normal international law we would have the right to deny such people entry. However, our membership of something called the Dublin III Agreement makes that financially and logistically very difficult.

Dublin III is an agreement amongst the 28 EU member states that determines that the EU member state responsible for asylum processing is the state through which a refugee enters the EU.

In theory this is an advantage for the UK given our geographical distance from the largest migration routes into the EU i.e. Greece, Italy, Malta and Spain. However, the Dublin III agreement requires the UK to return non-EU asylum seekers back to the country through which they entered the EU, as opposed to returning them to the last safe country they transited (generally France). Furthermore, the asylum seeker has a right of appeal against transferral and the UK is obliged to house them, clothe them, feed them and provide them with healthcare during the period of any appeal.

Dublin III creates conditions that undermine any deterrent to attempting to cross the English Channel and enter the UK unlawfully.

We must leave the Dublin III agreement.

In another stunning example of poor governance, the UK has no Integrated Border Management Strategy. The fact that we have no overarching strategy for our border management, as we also do not in healthcare, education, transport or pretty much anything else, is indicative of incompetence. In all these areas strategic frameworks that set common goals across multiple lines of operation and unify efforts towards achieving them are an urgent requirement. What we have instead is a patchwork of poorly organised and inadequately resourced agencies with no coherent framework in which to work.

There are many concrete steps that can be taken to manage immigration better.

5

REFUGEES, ECONOMIC MIGRANTS, HUMAN TRAFFICKING AND PEOPLE SMUGGLING

IF OUR PARLIAMENTARIANS, MEDIA AND COMMENTATORS DON'T KNOW THE DIFFERENCE BETWEEN THESE THINGS, HOW CAN THE PUBLIC BE EXPECTED TO UNDERSTAND WHAT IS HAPPENING AND HOW CAN EFFECTIVE SOLUTIONS POSSIBLY BE DESIGNED?

When talking about refugees, asylum seekers, immigrants, economic migrants, human trafficking and people smuggling, I am constantly amazed and frustrated by the inability of politicians, journalists, correspondents and commentators to understand the basics of what they are talking about.

Specifically, the majority seem entirely unaware of the difference between a refugee and a migrant, and the difference between people smuggling and human trafficking.

If our MPs' media and commentators don't know the difference, how can the public possibly know?

If we are ever, as a nation, to manage these things properly, give proper protection to those who really need it and go after those who knowingly cause or put people at risk of human suffering and death for a profit we must, of course, understand and agree what it is we're talking about.

This may help:

The United Nations High Commission for Refugees

(UNHCR) is the world's leading international authority on the subject of refugees. Below are the definitions it provides:

*"**Refugees** are persons fleeing armed conflict or persecution. There were 21.3 million of them worldwide at the end of 2015. Their situation is often so perilous and intolerable that they cross national borders to seek safety in nearby countries, and thus become internationally recognised as "refugees" with access to assistance from States, UNHCR, and other organisations. They are so recognised precisely because it is too dangerous for them to return home, and they need sanctuary elsewhere. These are people for whom denial of asylum has potentially deadly consequences. Refugees are defined and protected in international law. The 1951 Refugee Convention and its 1967 Protocol... remain[s] the cornerstone of modern refugee protection."*

*"**Migrants** choose to move not because of a direct threat of persecution or death, but mainly to improve their lives by finding work, or in some cases for education, family reunion, or other reasons. Unlike refugees who cannot safely return home, migrants face no such impediment to return. If they choose to return home, they will continue to receive the protection of their government."*

It is relevant and important to note that a migrant is therefore, by the United Nations definition, moving for practical or financial reasons and not because they cannot safely return home. When one realises this, it becomes obvious that the immigration debate in the UK is misinformed and does not understand the terminology that is being used. Migrants "choose" to come here. There are not forced or compelled to.

Because the international community recognises the plight of refugees, countries across the world manage refugee issues in accordance with international law, whereas they deal with migrants under their own, national, immigration policy.

Or most do...

The UK's refugee and immigration policy, legislation and processes, and indeed those of all EU member states, lie within the framework not only of international law, but also within an additional and complicated layer of EU treaties, laws, and regulations.

To remain within the European Union means to subordinate the country to EU immigration and asylum related policies and legislation.

That said, it is also a fact that even whilst in the EU, the British government is entirely free of EU immigration legislation when it comes to third country citizens (those from countries outside the EU) who arrive in the UK without transiting any other EU member state. Any attempt on the part of the government or Brexiteers to claim otherwise shows a distinct lack of understanding or is disingenuous, possibly dishonest.

The United Nations Office for Drugs and Crime (UNODC) is the guardian of the 'United Nations Convention against Transnational Organised Crime (UNTOC)' and the Protocols thereto. The UNODC assists States to prevent, suppress and punish trafficking in people. It defines the following:

. . .

Human Trafficking is *"the recruitment, transportation, transfer, harbouring or receipt of persons, by means of the threat or use of force or other forms of coercion, of abduction, of fraud, of deception, of the abuse of power or of a position of vulnerability or of the giving or receiving of payments or benefits to achieve the consent of a person having control over another person, for the purpose of exploitation. Exploitation shall include, at a minimum, the exploitation of the prostitution of others or other forms of sexual exploitation, forced labour or services, slavery or practices similar to slavery, servitude or the removal of organs."*

People Smuggling is the *"procurement, in order to obtain, directly or indirectly, a financial or other material benefit, of the illegal entry of a person into a State Party of which the person is not a national or a permanent resident."*

Incredibly, in the UK, our politicians, media and even some of our laws confuse and often conflate the two things.

How can MPs possibly address refugee, human trafficking and immigration issues if they haven't even managed to work out what it is that they are talking about?

Furthermore, there is a significantly loud and often abusive group of campaigners who like to create the impression that they are helping to protect the interests of refugees. They too, perhaps sometimes deliberately, often confuse or conflate the definitions of what a refugee is and what a migrant is. Their simplistic attitude and blind ignorance serve only to undermine the design of appropriate responses and helps absolutely nobody.

Often people smugglers knowingly puts people at risk of

death and are responsible for countless thousands of deaths worldwide. Just look at the drownings in the Mediterranean and the 39 dead Vietnamese people found in the back of a lorry in Essex in October 2019, for example.

Both people smuggling and human trafficking, particularly the former, can have far reaching and extremely serious implications.

They feed localised and transnational organised crime and corruption and frequently provide a source of funding for extremists, terrorists and rebels. People smuggling and human trafficking thereby undermine economies and fuel regional instability and conflict. This in turn frequently leads to international diplomatic, humanitarian and military intervention, drives further population movement and costs governments treasure and servicemen and women their blood.

People smugglers pose no lesser threat than terrorists do, and they should be dealt with similarly. The use of lethal force and the protocols for the use of such force against people smugglers is as appropriate as it is against a person plotting or conducting a terrorist attack.

6

ONE LAW FOR ALL

EQUALITY FOR ALL IN LAW, POLICING AND JUSTICE IS A PREREQUISITE FOR A STABLE, CONFIDENT AND SECURE SOCIETY

For policing and the rule of law to command respect they must be fair. They must apply and be applied equally to everyone, regardless of their background, culture or religion. Policing by consent requires people to agree to being policed - well done for figuring that out Sherlock - But if consent is withdrawn because policing is considered inequitable, we will all suffer increased crime and decreased security.

Regardless, recent years have seen an erosion of the principle of consent and fairness. The erosion has been caused by operational and political circumstances which, rather than being accepted and adapted to, should have been challenged by politicians, the police themselves and the public.

Operationally, tackling traveller camps and related crime, for example, is time and manpower intensive. Traveller related issues are the responsibility of several agencies who lack coordination - again we see the lack of strategic and integrated thinking as the root of our inability to effectively deal with a problem. It is often difficult to pin down the identity of individual travellers whose communities are involved in extensive minor criminality, extending through vehicle related crime to horrendous animal cruelty.

Criminal culpability involving members of traveller communities can be extremely difficult to evidence and successfully prosecute. Furthermore, search operations and arrests can be met with significant resistance.

The operational challenge is that the police simply don't have the resources to address traveller related problems effectively.

The political challenge is lack of preparedness on the part of politicians and the police to face the hassle that travellers create for them.

For these reasons, traveller communities are in the 'too difficult box' and able to live largely outside the law whilst the rest of us do not. This is an example of what I call inequitable policing.

It is a problem created by lack of political will, weak decision making, poor coordination, reduced police funding and, above all, a lack of concern for the communities and individuals that suffer because of 'traveller' behaviour. It is a problem, therefore, that could, given the political will and leadership, be addressed. So, why isn't it?

Likewise, the widespread and appalling abuse of animals owned by the traveller community is accepted because confronting it is too difficult for under resourced agencies. If you or I were to treat animals the way that some traveller communities do, there would be an outcry and we'd probably and rightly be prosecuted. They should be also.

Politically, however, perhaps the best examples of one rule for one community and another are these:

In the UK, the law states that animals being slaughtered must be stunned first, but the law also allows an exception.

Animals in the UK all have the arteries in their neck cut to 'bleed' them, however, Jewish and Muslim communities are exempt from the legal requirement to stun animals beforehand.

All Shechita (Jewish) and some Halal (Muslim) slaughter involves cutting the animal's throat without it being stunned beforehand.

Historically, non-stun slaughter and the rituals associated with it, evolved as the only available and therefore best method of slaughter. Indeed, at the time the Torah and the Koran (the Jewish and Islamic religious books) were laid down, no practical means of stunning was known or available. Had such means been available, one can imagine that religious law, as defined in those books, both of which highlight the need to respect the animal, would have made stunning a requirement.

In many parts of the world, there still exists no means of stunning an animal effectively before slaughter. In those areas and related societies, and in history, the non-stun slaughter of domestic animals is not only the only method available, but it has become customary. Because it involves the taking of a life, and the provision of food for which gratitude was shown - "for that which we are about to receive, may we be truly thankful" - such slaughter had and has in some societies a spiritual implication. It has therefore frequently been accompanied by religious ritual and, over time, has become intimately associated with certain religions. When adherents to those religions and people from those areas and societies come to the UK as immigrants their habit is naturally to continue to follow to the customs of their native society.

As anyone who has witnessed it, as the author has, non-stun slaughter unquestionably causes the animal concerned anguish and suffering. But whilst the consumption of 'pure' meat is a a laid down requirement laid down in Judaism and Islam, the non-stun slaughter of animals is not. It is rather a custom and habit to which some religions have become associated for the reasons I have explained.

The Torah five books of Moses do not prescribe the method of slaughter other than to state that the animal must be bled, nor do they forbid stun-slaughter. Only subsequent interpretation does that. Similarly, the Koran does not forbid stunned slaughter. So, why do we accept it? Even if stunning was prohibited by religion - which, as I say, it is not - we should surely not apply such a doctrine blindly, regardless of the suffering inflicted by doing so.

Here in the UK, there is no good reason to allow anyone, no matter what their background or religion is, to carry out the slaughter of an animal in an unnecessarily cruel manner simply because it is their habit or custom to do so.

Surely the law should apply equally to all and reflect the values and principles of the residents of these islands as one community, not as many.

Denmark, Luxembourg, Belgium, The Netherlands, Norway, Sweden and Switzerland have all banned non-stun slaughter slaughter so as to reduce the possibility of alarm, anxiety and distress. We in the UK should do the same.

My second example of the law and standards being applied inequitably to different communities in the UK is that of religious education and practices in our schools.

The Education watchdog Ofsted informed parliament in

2019, that it had not received the support it needs from the government to tackle discrimination in schools. This came as it emerged that an independent Muslim school Birmingham was denying girls the chance to have lunch until the boys had finished eating theirs and used "very discriminatory texts encouraging violence against women".

Ofsted told a parliamentary committee:

"Our inspectors are having to go out and make some quite tricky judgements when there are those potential clashes [with schools] with protected characteristics. We don't feel like we get the support we need from the rest of government in pushing that forward."

Ofsted has also said many independent schools repeatedly fail the independent school standards on equalities and education issues.

"We really do think that quicker action needs to be taken against schools who we have persistently identified as being 'inadequate'."

Schools run by religious or ethnic communities create a sensitive problem for regulators and politicians alike. This has come about because of fear, on the part of politicians, of being labelled 'racist' or prejudiced and a resultant lack of moral and ethical decisiveness.

The fact is that we, in the UK, have led the global drive for equal rights and an end to discrimination largely by example and through our foreign diplomatic engagements. At home, in our own society, over the last century or more, people have made massive sacrifices and achieved great advances in this cause.

Yet, now, it seems that many of our politicians and some activists are prepared to undermine, compromise and even reverse those achievements by allowing people from other societies an exemption from having to apply them here.

Applying one rule for some and another for others is the surest way to create, rather than remove barriers to integration and trust; it is a certain way to undermine standards in social behaviour and to increase tensions between communities.

So, why are exemptions to the law and rules permitted in the case of certain religions or cultures?

I can only imagine that it is a lack of moral and ethical courage on the part of politicians who are frightened of being criticised by an irresponsible, social liberal media that thrives off scandal and loves to sensationalise any issue rather than praise decisions that strengthen the cohesiveness of society. Such criticism would, in turn, potentially lose the politicians votes and ultimately damage their career, so they choose not to act.

There is nothing prejudicial about applying laws and regulations equally. Quite the opposite. It is prejudicial not to.

How have we allowed a situation to evolve in which the unequal and therefore unfair application of laws and regulations is in some way acceptable or expected? Who are the people who have submitted to this erosion of the rule of law? Who are the people who advocate it? Are we, as a nation, one community made up of people with diverse backgrounds, happy and content with this? Or does it worry us? After all, if today one part of the community is advantaged by inequitable application of the law, tomorrow it may suffer as a result of it.

And let us remember something that almost everyone

agrees on, inequality is one of the most significant drivers of dissent, bitterness, crime and social division.

So, we see in this yet another example of the poor quality of our MPs. Can we say their lack of moral and ethical courage and their frequently partisan approach contributes towards cultural/religious divisions in society and undermines the rule of law and policing by consent? I believe we can say that, yes.

POLICING & PRISONS

Direct central government funding for policing fell by 30% between 2010/11 and 2018/19, during the Conservative governments of Cameron (whilst Theresa May was Home Secretary) and May.

The Conservative government allowed Police and Crime Commissioners to mitigate the impact of cuts by raising money directly from other sources. The main source is an increase in the council tax precept, which you and I pay for in addition to paying income tax. These 'mitigating' measures accounted for, the net loss to policing under the Conservatives between 2011 and 2019 still fell by an outrageous 19%.

The 2015 Police Spending Review promised to "protect overall police spending in real terms over the Spending Review period" 2019/20. That promise was not acted upon.

In contradiction to that pledge, central government funding fell in real terms. The government reduced its expenditure whilst pledging to keep the police budget at its present level *so long as you pay more council tax*. Even then, it doesn't bridge the gap.

Conservative government policy between 2011 and 2019 was to outsource the management of prisons and the Probation Service. There is no question that the policy has been an unmitigated failure, yet it has been pursued persistently because of blind adherence to conservative doctrine. Much the same has occurred in national healthcare and many administrative functions within the Ministry of Defence and other government departments.

Violence in prisons nearly doubled in the ten years between 2007 and 2017. Assaults on staff rose from 3,386 to 7,437. Prisoner on prisoner assaults rose from 11,696 to 19,756. The rate was gradually falling under Labour and then rose rapidly under the Conservative government.

With an expanding population and rising violent crime, can these policies be described in any way as common sense? Of course, they cannot. So, why pursue them? It is because our politicians lack the vision, initiative, intellect, strategic acumen and will to do anything other than blindly adhere to doctrine, whether it be liberal economics, socialism or any other. Take the guiding railway tracks of doctrine and ideology away and they have no idea where to go or what to do. Such people are inadequate when it comes to leading the country. Even if they are brilliant at something else, they should not be in parliament or government. They should put their vanity and egos to one side and stick to what they are good at.

7

TERRORISM, THE TREASON ACT & THE FAILURE TO ACT

AN EXAMPLE OF HOW POLITICAL TIMIDITY THREATENS NOT ONLY PUBLIC CONFIDENCE, BUT ALSO PUBLIC SAFETY.

In a very British way, we have extant laws that date back to the Middle Ages and yet remain useful, if only rarely applied. One of the oldest of these is the Treason Act 1351.

Section II of the Treason Act 1351 defines what offences shall be adjudged Treason:

• *Compassing the Death of the King, Queen, or their eldest Son;*

• *violating the Queen, or the King's eldest Daughter unmarried, or his eldest Son's Wife;*

• *levying War; adhering to the King's Enemies; killing the Chancellor, Treasurer, or Judges in Execution of their Duty.*

The Act goes on to state that it also applies...

"If a Man do levy War against our Lord the King in his Realm, or be adherent to the King's Enemies in his Realm, giving to them Aid and Comfort in the Realm, or elsewhere..."

This clearly covers any British citizen supporting or fighting for ISIS/Daesh, Al Qaeda etc, here in the UK, "*in his Realm*", or abroad *"elsewhere"*. Such terrorist organisations are clearly enemies of the UK and therefore of the sovereign.

A British citizen preparing, supporting or conducting a terrorist attack in the UK or against sovereign (national) interests elsewhere, or in any way supporting or fighting for an "enemy of Realm" could quite reasonably be considered as adhering to them and "giving them aid and comfort". So, there would almost certainly be a treason charge to answer, even if the person did not actually pick up a gun and was instead involved in a supporting capacity, such as funding, providing expertise, logistical assistance, information or equipment.

Other offences could be applied in such cases, such as murder and those covered by the Terrorism Act 2006. The later includes encouragement of terrorism, dissemination of terrorist publications, preparation of terrorist acts, participating in terrorist training, attendance at a place of terrorist training etc.

The decision as to what charge to make against a terrorist or enemy of the realm, in other words, the decision as to whether or not to use the Treason Act, the Terrorism Act or another appropriate Act, is one for the Crown Prosecution Service and government/Home Office policy and guidelines. In making that decision, gaining a successful prosecution must be a paramount consideration, but three is a politically motivated reticence to use the Treason Act. It conjures up the impression of state rule of law power as an unambiguous, unforgiving and immovable force. However, this impression is also a very good reason to employ the Treason Act. Politicians simply have to have the courage to allow the justice system to do so

Do other arguments exist for the Treason Act be used in cases where it can be successfully applied to obtain a prosecution?

Yes, two:

Firstly, there is, quite simply, no more demeaning a label, no term more condemnatory of character, loyalty and integrity than that of "Traitor".

British citizens who fight for, or support the enemies of the realm as terrorists, or in any other way, are not freedom fighters, they are not idealists, they are not potential martyrs, they are beyond doubt the most despicable, reprehensible and lowest of criminals; they are traitors. If they are combatants; if they use or support the use or threat of lethal force in a practical way, they must either be killed on the battlefield or charged with Treason as the traitors are.

Secondly, the full power of the state; the unambiguous, unforgiving and immovable application of the force of law is entirely appropriate in the case of a British citizen guilty of "War against our Lord the King in his Realm, or adherent to the King's Enemies in his Realm, giving to them Aid and Comfort in the Realm, or elsewhere..."

Treason in such cases must carry a statutory life sentence. Such a sentence must truly mean life i.e. that those found guilty of treason must never be eligible for release from prison for any reason whatsoever. They will die in prison.

It would be entirely reasonable to hold a national referendum on whether the death sentence should be an option in cases involving entirely unambiguous crimes of treason. An example would be that of the killing, in May 2013, of Fusilier Lee Rigby, a British soldier in the Royal Regiment of Fusiliers. The two disgusting, traitorous murderers, in that case, Michael Adebolajo and Michael Adebowale, both made the conscious and deliberate decision to attack their own society, as represented by Fusilier Rigby, to undermine it and aid its destruction. Furthermore, their gratuitous act of violence was captured on film. There is no question of new information or advances in forensic science at some point in the future proving their innocence; there is no ambiguity whatsoever in this case and nor will there ever be. Should the British taxpayer be asked to pay for the accommodation, food, healthcare, education, training, welfare and other perks that they receive during incarceration? I pose the question.

National leaders, parliament, the courts, Crown Prosecution Service and police all need to respond to crimes committed by British citizens and that are intended to give enemies of the realm aid or comfort for what they are: acts of treason. Those committing them are traitors, nothing more, nothing less. That is the label they should be given.

8

DISENFRANCHISEMENT OF THE POPULATION

THE DOMINANCE OF PROCESSES, PROCEDURES, SYSTEMS AND THE DECREASING RELEVANCE OF PEOPLE

How many people truly believe that politicians listen to them? How many believe that anything they say is considered when decisions are made that affect the community and environment they live in?

According to the Electoral Reform Society, two thirds of people (67%), feel they have very few or no opportunities to inform and influence decisions made by MPs.

At the local level, we have all seen it; the housing developments in our back yard or the adjacent fields, that we have opposed but that go ahead regardless; the buildings that destroy the character of a community, but are none the less allowed to be built on a scale and in a style that is utterly unsympathetic.

Communities raise issues that are never addressed. Attempts by developers and planning authorities to mitigate the impact of developments or to seek compromise are unfortunately far too rare.

Local councils dominated by one party, frequently run by a character of a dictatorial nature and a 'behind closed doors' cabinet system which obstructs transparency and therefore accountability, create a well deserved and hugely negative impression of politicians and politics at all levels. The loss of public trust in our political system that results is incredibly negative and damaging to our democracy. The common failure of MPs to support and represent the interests and concerns of their constituents over those of their councils in such cases, particularly when the MP belongs to the same party that leads the council, undermines public faith in our political class even further.

At the national level, nothing demonstrates the disenfranchisement of the population more clearly than the delay in implementing the 2016 Brexit referendum result and the open resistance to that implementation on the part of so many MPs.

Under Prime Minister May, Cabinet ministers and parliamentarians simply seemed not to give a damn that the nation voted, by a majority of over one and a quarter million, to leave the European Union.

In a clear attempt to boost the party's fortunes by tapping into the 'Remain' vote and in total defiance of the referendum vote, the Liberal Democrats under Jo Swinson adopted remaining in the European Union as their centrepiece national policy.

The Labour Party under Jeremy Corbyn adopted the bizarre policy of wanting to negotiate a deal with the EU in order to put that deal to the British people in a second referendum during which they would campaign against that deal and for remaining in the EU. In its practical application this was the Labour Party also campaigning against implementation of the 2016 referendum result.

The individual opinions of some politicians, particularly

on the left and the so called 'liberal' centre, are very openly that we should not leave the EU despite a democratic instruction from the British people to do so. These politicians are so contemptuous of the British people as to do everything they possibly can to obstruct and prevent our departure.

Imagine if you would, what would happen if they tried to obstruct the implementation of a general election result. As a matter of democratic principle, the parliamentary Brexit debacle has been no different.

And which party has led the charge on sticking two fingers up at the referendum result? The Liberal Democrats. The language from elected LibDem politicians was appalling and illustrates my point.

Irina von Wiese MEP @IrinavonWiese · 24 Jul
A racist, xenophobic, sexist liar is now Prime Minister of the United Kingdom.

As a patriot and a European, my heart aches for our great country. We can do better than @BorisJohnson.

Now more than ever, we must fight to keep Britain in the #EU. We can #stopBrexit together.

Is it any wonder that the voters of 2019 question whether or not politicians care what they think or how they cast their votes?

But the system is not only compromised, it is broken.

I was involved in a case in which a community heritage preservation association opposed Network Rail's proposed to close a historic railway branch line. During the public consultation process and in its submissions to the Department for Transport, the heritage association in question blew apart the case for closure. None the less, following a failed appeal, the closure went ahead. On enquiring with the Department for Transport and the Office of Rail and Road as to why the facts of the case appeared not to have been considered in the first instance or during the appeal, they were told:

"We are only permitted to assess the appeal based on whether the correct process has been applied"

The question was then asked: "so the facts of the case were not considered?" The answer was:

"We are not empowered to make a judgement based on the information put forward by the parties unless it relates to the process".

So, there we have it, only the process matters, the facts do not. Frankly, if the facts don't matter, then clearly people have no influence and the impact on their lives is irrelevant. What an indictment of our system as it presently stands.

The process in so many of these things involves public consultations of various sorts. This might reasonably be taken to imply that the authorities have an interest in what we have to say; that authorities are expected to listen; that people have a voice that will be heard. We assume, or at we least hope, that our voice may have some degree of influence.

The bitter truth, however, is that all too often the public consultation process is simply there to make us *think* that our opinion matters. The truth is that individuals and communities rarely have any influence on decisions that impact upon them. Unaccountable officials can point to legislation, regulations, permitted exceptions and correctly completed consultation processes to say: "look we did everything by the book".

Public opinion matters little in present day public consultation unless it is of such a scale and so well organised that it poses a political threat to those in power.

Processes have also crept subtly but decisively into all areas of the administration.

In all areas, staff are instructed to doggedly apply procedures and guidelines. Indeed they are trained to do so, rather than to use them with discretion and to apply commons sense.

The interests, concerns and unique circumstances of individuals are trumped by the administration's determination to protect itself.

Processes and procedures enable the 'system' to absolve itself of the blame for errors: "oh, but the procedures were applied".

As procedures, check lists and systems increase, so the importance of the individual or the community, and their relevance to and influence on decision making, decreases.

We know who the politicians are, but we should demand that the faceless individuals who created these processes, that were never described in any manifesto, are also held to account.

Were we ever consulted by the politicians who passed the legislation that now means we have no say and that, even if we can express ourselves, allows institutions, organisations, developers and local councils to dodge around our objections?

Where is the transparency so vital to a healthy, functioning democratic system?

Why do our politicians allow such situation?

I suspect self interest, out of touch 'bubble politics' and a lack of grasp and strategic acumen are to blame.

Why do we, the voters, fail to hold our elected representatives and political parties to account and instead allow them to erode our relevance and sense of worth? Why do people vote for the same old parties and accept the same appalling lack of respect, performance and care?

The British people are not militant by nature or character.

We avoid confrontation. However, we have to demand a new attitude in politics. We must demand vision, inspiration, integrity and altruism from our political parties and class. If things do not improve, I believe that a new, non-violent revolution will come to pass. It will happen when someone devises a very British, non-populist way of carrying it out.

9

ECONOMICS AND THE SACRIFICE OF THE POPULATION ON THE ALTER OF IDEOLOGY

INADEQUATE POLITICIANS HAVE THEIR EYE CONSTANTLY ON THE REFEREE RATHER THAN ON THE BALL OR THE GOAL

The government's income, its revenue, for the financial year 2020 is expected to be an incredible £811.4 billion. The British tax payer is contributing £268.3bn in income tax, £143.4bn in National insurance, £345.3bn in indirect taxes like VAT, and business is contributing £63.4bn.

So what? We have to pay for stuff, right?

But wait a moment. Since the conservative government came to power in 2010, National insurance has risen to its highest ever level and someone who earns £25,000 now pays around £44 more than they did in 2014.

Since 2010, government income tax revenue has gone up from £541bn to £792bn. That's an annual increase in revenue for the government of £251bn in nine years!

But the figures that I find most interesting are those of overall public spending. Public spending has increased from £673bn in 2010, when the Conservatives came to power, to £821bn in 2019.

In other words, government expenditure has increased by £148bn in a year (that is more than our entire national education and defence budgets combined), but, as we all know, there have been swathing cuts to public services: policing cut by 20%; local government cut in some areas by up to 50%.

Policing, local government, education per pupil and other areas have all been subject to significant cuts, yet we're spending £148bn more. So, where is all this money going?

Well, let's look at healthcare.

Spending on healthcare increased from £117bn in 2010 to £153bn in 2019. That is an increase of £36bn, a huge amount roughly equivalent to the entire defence budget. The Conservative government under Boris Johnson promised a further £20bn which would mean an overall increase to the NHS budget over the last nine year of 65%. But doctor's surgeries are closing, waiting times for beds, operations and for the arrival of an ambulance are climbing; positive patient outcomes are not. What is going on?

The fact is that the Conservative government has massively increased the amount spent on profit-driven healthcare companies to £8.77bn in 2017-18.

Furthermore, the twenty hospital Private Funding Initiative (PFI) schemes in London cost £2.7bn to build, but require payments totalling £20.2bn from the fifteen NHS trusts that are involved in these contracts.

Around 100 NHS hospitals nationwide have been built under the PFI scheme. The total ongoing cost to the budgets of the NHS trusts involved as is unknown. Ownership of these hospitals has undergone a dramatic shift over the last decade, and nine out of ten are now effectively owned by international investment funds and, in case it escaped the attention of our politicians, international investment funds are in the business of making profits. They are doing so from taxpayers money; taxpayers money that we, the taxpayers, expect to be paid into our healthcare system, not the pockets of company Directors (many of whom already earn vastly more than the Prime Minister, generals and most senior civil servants) and shareholders.

Similar things have been happening in other Pubic sectors. Public funds are going into commercial, profit making companies to run prisons, probation services and Highways management to name but a few.

More and more services are being outsourced to private commercial, profit making organisations. Figures for how much public (taxpayer) money finds its way into the dividends made to directors and shareholders are elusive. But it certainly runs into the billions.

Some supporters of outsourcing argue that the expenditure is worth it in order to bring in greater expertise and improve the quality of delivery through competition. But in most cases, this is frankly rubbish.

Some of the dividends and bonuses paid to senior staff of commercial organisations being funded by the tax payer are disgusting.

The massive salaries paid to some staff and consultants of commercial providers generally outstrip that paid to public workers. So we end up losing public staff e.g. doctors and nurses from the NHS, who have been trained and given experience by the NHS, to commercial agencies. Those agencies are then awarded contracts to supply staff to the NHS. Forgive me if I don't quite grasp the sense in this.

Can anyone possibly say that our prisons, management of which is now outsourced as a matter of general practice, are better for it? Prisoner on prisoner and prisoner on staff assaults almost doubled between 2011 and 2017. Drug use in prisons has exploded and a lot of organised crime on the streets is run from, inside prisons.

It is not rocket science. If public money is spent on state providers, then that money should go further than if shareholder dividends and huge director salaries and bonuses have to be deducted from it.

There is, of course, the idea that private providers in a competitive market place are compelled by market forces to provide better value for money than non-competitive state providers, but does the performance of our prisons, army recruitment or railways bear this out? No, it does not.

No doubt, in specific, particularly technical areas, commercial providers may be in a unique position to raise the quality of public service output and value for money, but these are the exception. So, I do not blindly rule out the employment of specialist providers or consultants. But, on grounds of efficiency, value for money, public service and the national economy, I do reject the principle that government should divulge itself of delivery as a matter of general practice.

I also reject dogmatic outsourcing for another extremely important reason. The government must be democratically accountable for the delivery and performance of public services (health, education, policing, defence, prisons etc) and for strategic national infrastructure (power, rail etc). If the planning, development, operation, delivery, maintenance and efficiency of those things are in the hands of private, commercial organisations how do we, the public, know who is responsible for what? Who is accountable? And even if we blame our politicians, how can they respond if they've been locked into legally binding contracts with private contractors. And even if they could remove the contractor, who would then deliver the service? If we, the people, blame the companies to which the outsourcing contracts have been given, we cannot vote them out; we cannot remove them. The principle of democratic accountability is broken. And remember, many commercial suppliers of publicly funded public services have foreign owners, shareholders and management. The rail franchise operator Arriva, for example, is a subsidiary of Deutsche Bahn, the German State owned national rail operator.

Why, when there is concern over the national security implications of the Chinese State owned telecoms giant Huawei being awarded the contract for rolling out the national 5G mobile and internet infrastructure, is the government even contemplating it?

Furthermore, when it is argued that a commercial provider will provide greater value for money, it must be remembered that value for money for a shareholder of such an organisation means reducing costs and increasing profits. In public service, it should be about reducing costs and increasing public benefit and this should be reflected within the organisation's planning. The two organisations, public and private, generally seek a different set of outcomes and their operations are designed and prioritised accordingly.

Take railways for example. A commercial rail operator is primarily concerned about the service it runs being profitable. In other words, it is about paying shareholder dividends. A state owned rail operator, on the other hand, is able to sacrifice profits to empower the broader economy and thereby provide second and third order benefits for the greater good: more business start-ups, lower business costs, fewer relocations, greater access to markets, easier commuting, more jobs and regional regeneration - the list is long.

Why on Earth would a private commercial rail operator be worried about enabling other businesses to thrive and grow, even when doing so would provide a much greater overall benefit to the nation? Their performance is not judged on the greater good of the national economy, or passenger satisfaction, it is judged by its shareholders who are focused narrowly on the return on their investment and who have no interest in empowering the broader economy.

Are we, the taxpayer getting better value for money as a result of the policies of privatisation and outsourcing? I don't think so. Dogmatic adherence to any fiscal or economic philosophy is dangerous, yet both the Conservative and the Labour parties are responsible for doing exactly this.

Of course, nationalisation can be carried too far. In the right conditions, market forces create competition that on turn encourages innovation, pushes up standards and drives down consumer costs. So, government direction should apply only in limited only areas of strategically crucial provision such as healthcare, education, national transport infrastructure etc. Nationalisation of communications or of manufacturing would be entirely inappropriate. The former would potentially facilitate state interference in personal privacy, communications and freedom of speech and the later would create inertia in competitive commerce.

What do you think?

10

THE GREAT BREXIT BETRAYAL & THE THREAT TO OUR DEMOCRACY

IS IT THE CROWN, THE PEOPLE OR THEIR PARLIAMENT THAT IS SOVEREIGN? PERHAPS THE ANSWER TO BREXIT LIES IN THE ANSWER TO THIS QUESTION

There are two 'betrayals'.

The first is the refusal of parliament to accept and implement the 2016 referendum result to leave the European Union. This is a betrayal of trust.

This betrayal of trust has created parliamentary chaos. This chaos has been fed and exploited by specifically Remain supporting and some Marxist parliamentarians, in particular the leadership of the Labour Party, aided by arguably the most partisan Speaker since the 17th century, to bring about major constitutional change. These subversives, because that is what they are, seek to establish a veto over the exercise of prerogative powers by the Executive and to institute a dangerous constitutional precedent that parliamentary sovereignty trumps that of the people who elect its members. This is the second betrayal; the betrayal of our our historic, constitutional monarchy and democracy, whereby Parliament legislates and the Executive (government) directs the resources of State under the Crown.

The people select individuals to represent them, their

interests and those of the nation in parliament. The people do this through the process of election. Members of Parliament are elected and appointed to their office by the people. In that way, they can be said draw their authority to legislate and hold the government to account from the people. The people, not parliament, are surely sovereign in this respect.

Parliament's function in legislating is the greatest and most important of its roles and, of course, includes legislating concerning finance and the raising of taxes. In this respect, and only in this respect, in my view, is Parliament, as an institution, not as a collection of its members, sovereign. Parliament raises taxes to provide the Crown - the State - with the means to conduct business.

There is another task that Parliament should carry out, but that in recent years has failed to with any effectiveness whatsoever. It is a function relevant to the Brexit debate and the broader context of national politics and democracy. That function is one of informing and educating the people. It is the responsibility of Parliament to ensure that the people are aware of and understand the context, facts and implications concerning any subject on which they may base a decision as to how to vote; it is a function that should result in informed electoral choice. This function is fundamental to democracy. If people are not informed, are informed partially, incorrectly or deliberately misinformed, it stands to reason that they are unable to make a properly informed decision and there can therefore be no effective democracy. It may be argued that not only has Parliament failed in this respect but that it, and the parties represented within it, have deliberately done so for the purposes on manipulating public opinion.

On a brief tangent, it must be said that the electorate must also be willing to receive or seek complete and objectively presented information. Tribalism encouraged by political parties, and group think, encouraged by social media bubbles, has done much to erode the ability of the public to think objectively.

Back to the main point... It is important to where the respective powers lie in Parliament in order analysing and understand the threat to our system posed by naive Remainers working in alliance with the Marxist left of the Labour leadership.

The sovereignty of government, as the Executive, differs from that of Parliament.

The Cabinet, which is the executive committee of government, draws its authority to direct the resources commanded by the Crown not from the people, but from the Sovereign, as representing the Crown. In this sense, the Crown is sovereign.

So, where do the people come into the Brexit equation?

In 2016 Parliament opined that the question as to whether or not the United Kingdom should leave the European Union or remain a member state was of such great importance that responsibility for deciding the matter should be returned to the people.

In passing the EU Referendum Act 2015, Parliament formally asked the people to decide whether the UK should leave the EU or not, thereby surrendering its authority on the matter to the people. In doing so, it recognised the people as sovereign.

Following the passing of the Referendum Act, the Government launched a campaign to assist the people in making their decision. In the campaign in the run up to the 'Great Brexit Referendum', the Government spent £9m of taxpayers' money on a booklet that was sent to every household in the UK. The purpose of the booklet was clearly communicated by its title:

"Why the Government believes that voting to remain in the European Union is the best decision for the UK".

The booklet put the case simply and clearly for remaining in the European Union. It encouraged the population to vote to remain.

Significantly, however, that same booklet also stated:

This is *"A once in a generation decision."*

And that:

"This is your decision. The Government will implement what you decide."

The people rejected the government's advice and the referendum resulted in a win for the Leave campaign. 17.4m people, a majority of over one and a quarter million, voted to leave the EU.

Yet, despite the Parliament's recognition of the right of the people to decide the Brexit question an d despite the Government's promise that it would *"...implement what you decide"*, 3 years later in June 2019, the country found itself no nearer to leaving the European Union that it was on 24th June 2016.

According to Peter Bone MP (Conservative), Theresa May stated as many as 108 times in the House of Commons that *"the UK will leave the EU on the 29th March 2019".*

Despite her repeated assurances, we did not. What impact did Theresa May think that would have on public trust and confidence in politics and politicians?

A great many leading politicians, who campaigned to remain in the EU stated very clearly that *"a vote to leave means leaving the single market and the customs union"*; that *"if we leave there is no guarantee of a deal"*; that *"If we leave, Britain would have less of a voice on the global stage".* Then these same people had the temerity to say that the people didn't know what they were voting for. Of course we did. They, in campaigning to persuade us, the people to vote to Remain, made sure we knew what we were voting for.

Furthermore, these same 'Remain' politicians: Grieve, Benn, Cameron, Blair, Osborne, Soubry amongst others told the British people that the referendum result would be respected and implemented; that the UK would leave the EU. But since the referendum result, they've done nothing but oppose its implementation.

What do these individuals think the people take them for? They have done nothing but undermine the integrity of the offices they hold and the reputation of the House of Commons and politicians in general.

Why on Earth do we elect such people to Westminster? We do vote for them so, perhaps, we are to blame.

How do such people ever become parliamentary candidates? Surely all political parties have serious questions to ask themselves about their candidate selection criteria.

We the electorate must demand better candidates from our political parties; we must demand honesty, transparency and political integrity from our representatives and we must move to deselect those who abuse or take for granted our political trust and support.

The fact is that the rightful and perfectly reasonable expectations of the 17.4m who voted to leave the European Union, have been raised and dashed far too many times. Even once is a time too many.

The public trust placed in our politicians to implement the referendum result as promised has been betrayed.

Many people who voted to remain in the EU are also flabbergasted. They are worried by the refusal of so many politicians to accept the referendum result. They understand that democracy relies on the agreement of those that lose a vote to accept its result. Too many politicians have refused to accept the referendum result and ordinary people on all sides of the debate rightly see this as damaging to our democratic institutions and system.

People are asking themselves, whether or not our present political class can be entrusted with the authority to manage the nation's interests.

I have expressed the view that the people are sovereign, but are they?

The sovereignty of the people over parliament should never have been a question in the Brexit debate. None the less, the discussion in parliament has moved from "should the UK leave the EU or not?" - that question was decided by the people - to "where does sovereignty lie? Does it lie with parliament or with the people?" Can parliament overrule the decision of the people?

Prime Minister Johnson believes as I do, that sovereignty lies with the people and that parliament legislates with the consent of the people, much as or law enforcement officers conduct 'policing by consent'.

However, MPs who believe passionately that the UK should remain a member of the EU argue that parliament is sovereign and that it is therefore for MPs to decide the matter as to whether we do leave and, if so, the manner in which we do. At the time of writing, some national politicians are openly arguing that we should not leave the EU at all. The official policy of the Liberal Democrat Party is to revoke our decision to leave. They refuse to accept the will of the people as determined in a lawful democratic vote requested by parliament. In so refusing, far from uniting the country as they claim, they encourage political polarisation and perpetuate uncertainty.

The question as to where sovereignty lies is perhaps the most serious constitutional issue to arise since the 1640s. The outcome may have massive implications. Although the consequences will be less dramatic than the English Civil Wars, they may, in the long term, be no less significant.

A conclusion that parliament is sovereign, would establish a worrying precedent regarding the democratic authority of the people to direct and hold parliament to account. It would imply that Parliament may overrule or interpret a national plebiscite. It could, potentially, have huge consequences for the implementation of, for example, general election results. If parliament is free to decide whether or not a referendum result should be implemented, why should it not also be suggest that it is competent by precedent to decide whether or not a general election result should be implemented? There may be a difference in law, but in terms of democratic principle and sovereignty, there is not.

The likes of Labour Party Leader, Jeremy Corbyn and Shadow Chancellor, John MacDonnell have used the Brexit debate to argue passionately for parliamentary sovereignty over the decisions of government. This ignores the fact that Parliament is not the government. Parliament holds the government to account on behalf of the people. Corbyn, McDonnell and their supporters would have parliament usurp many functions of government. But then, who will hold parliament to account, bearing in mind that Corbyn, McDonnell and others are also argue that parliament is sovereign and the people are not?

The partial, gradual or complete usurpation or vetoing of the executive decisions of government would make government, at least partly, redundant. Not only would this drastically reduce oversight and accountability, it would also severely undermine the constitutional role of the Monarch on whose authority the government directs the resources to govern.

This debate, somewhat masked by the parliamentary debate on Brexit, is of the most serious importance. An example is the implication of a ruling by the Speaker of the House of Commons, John Bercow.

Bercow ruled that the Benn-Burt Bill did not require Royal Consent. The Bill is important as it compelled the Prime Minister to not only request, but also to agree to an extension of the Article 50 notice and a postponement of the date of the UK's departure from the EU. The Bill also passed some of the executive decision making powers involved in setting a date for the UK's departure from the EU to the EU itself.

Why is this significant?

It is significant for two reasons: it interferes directly with 'prerogative' and, in doing so, it weakens the bedrock of our nation's governance and much of the reason that why we, as a nation, have possessed the advantage of flexible and responsive government in times of national crisis of foreign affairs and defence.

Prerogative powers are held by the Monarch and used by government ministers. They may be used without the consent of the Commons or Lords. Such powers include the power to conclude treaties and agreements with foreign powers. The constitution and parliamentary procedures require the speaker to rule on whether or not a Bill put before parliament may interfere with Prerogative and, if so, to rule that Royal Consent i.e. the consent of the government, is required before the Bill is heard (debated and voted upon).

Despite the Benn-Burt Bill interfering with Crown Prerogative, Speaker Bercow, in ruling that it did not require Consent, set a precedent that potentially handicaps the ability of present or future governments to conduct foreign policy without the permission of parliament. Furthermore, Bercow's ruling establishes a precedent on which parliament could challenge the constitutional powers of both the government and the monarch, weakening the bedrock of our nation's constitutional governance.

Here it is noteworthy that Bercow stated, when announcing his departure from office to the House of Commons, that his aim had been to increase the powers of parliament over those of the government. He succeeded, and in succeeding has significantly weakened the ability of the Executive to manage the affairs of the State effectively and efficiently. Of course, the country will not notice this on a day to day basis, but the impact, whilst subtle, will be hugely significant and negative in terms of Britain's ability to project onto the global stage in all areas from trade, through security, to the environment.

The Labour Party's refusal to support Prime Minister Johnson in implementing Brexit on 31st October, a date that parliament had previously agreed to, directly challenged the referendum result and therefore the sovereignty of the people. Labour Party Leader, Jeremy Corbyn and his Shadow Chancellor, John MacDonnell, have both argued passionately, along with others, that parliament is sovereign. Here it is perhaps relevant to note that both men are Marxists, or at least have very strong Marxist sympathies.

This is important because Marxism emphasises public

ownership of the means of production, distribution and markets; in other words, state control. Marxist regimes invariably strive to centralise decision making and are notoriously resistant to public scrutiny and accountability. They seek to remove or politicise the institutions that provide balance and prevent excess in British politics. That is why they argue, for example, for the abolition of the Monarchy. In that context, it can be seen that there is an inherent risk in upsetting the balance of sovereignty and placing executive powers in the hands of parliament.

It is vital that the balance of power involving the Monarchy, Government, Parliament and the People is not upset. If the debate being played out between Leave and Remain politicians results in an acceptance of the sovereignty of Parliament over both the People and the Executive (the Crown), the balance of power that prevents political abuse and authoritarianism will be fundamentally and irrevocably disturbed.

So, there is a great deal more at stake in the Brexit debate than simply whether or not the UK leaves the EU and how. The debate seems to have been high-jacked by those who seek to bring about massive constitutional change and they must not succeed.

It is crucial for the maintenance of our democratic system that the sovereignty of the people is established, that the prerogative powers of the Monarch and the Executive are maintained and that those who argue for parliamentary sovereignty over that of the people and the executive are defeated.

The failure of MPs to support the implementation of the 2016 referendum result and the argument as to whether parliament or the people are sovereign have hugely undermined already very low public trust and confidence in politicians. They threaten to do yet greater harm.

In all likelihood, the UK will, at some point, leave the European Union, quite possibly by the time you read this book. However, the damage to public trust and confidence, done by Theresa May's prevarication will take many years to undo, even given fair winds and a following sea.

If we are to address this problem and safeguard our constitutional order, we have to first make some effort to understand why it is that Parliament has let the country down so badly regarding Brexit.

There are at least three things to consider.

Firstly, our present Westminster political class is incompetent. They cannot lead. They have no idea how to lead. The ubiquitous 'career politicians' lack real-world experience and possess, in some cases anyway, academic ability rather than intelligence and common sense. They have been brought up in an age in which processes predominate and are therefore lost and indecisive in the fluid, changing and unpredictable environment of a national crisis that requires unconventional thought and imagination to solve. In any such moment of complex national crisis, or indeed in any but a steady-state environment, they are the wrong people, in the wrong place, at the wrong time. This takes us back to the candidate selection standards and processes employed by political parties.

Secondly, ministers are supported by a civil service that is institutionally averse to leaving the EU. It has been conditioned over time by circumstances to believe, falsely, that the UK cannot thrive outside the EU's governance framework. It is all they know. Institutionally, the civil service finds it difficult to envision an alternative framework and is insecure at the prospect of the present one being removed. This is explored in chapter 15, *"The Civil Service & the Mystery of the Unaccountable Mandarins".*

Thirdly, Westminster politicians have forgotten that whilst we expect them to exercise their own conscience, we elect them to represent our will, to act in the best interests of the nation, not their own. Occasionally this means that they have to subordinate their own opinions to ours. This concept and the competence, or otherwise, of politicians, is explored in Chapter 13, *"Westminster's Village Idiots"*

11

BREXIT & THE INCOMPETENT NEGOTIATOR

A STORY OF POLITICAL COWARDICE, NEGLIGENCE AND APPALLING LEADERSHIP; THE REAL STORY BEHIND THE £39 'BUNG' TO THE EUROPEAN COMMISSION AND WHY NORTHERN IRELAND SHOULD NEVER HAVE BEEN AN ISSUE.

The May government's handling of the Brexit negotiations was a shocking catalogue of incompetence and failure.

Firstly, following the 2016 referendum, the decision that the UK should submit notice of its intention to leave the European Union under Article 50 of the Treaty of the European Union, was made by a majority vote in parliament.

The submission of notice of our departure from the EU then started the clock ticking on the two years set by European Union law for preparing for that departure. The incompetence in this was that the government set the clock ticking and therefore launched negotiations before having a clue as to what its objectives for the negotiations were. They entered negotiations without any defined end state, without a plan and so, of course, totally unprepared.

Secondly, when, after significant delay, the government finally issued its so called 'position papers', they turned out to be nothing more than a vague series of wish lists. These papers, we were told, laid out the UK's negotiating position.

They did no such thing. It was no wonder that EU officials were tearing their hair out and had no idea what the UK government wanted – the UK government itself had no idea.

Here, before going to the third point, it is worth disappearing down a rabbit hole to understand why the UK, deliberately, entered the negotiations without any objectives.

There is a prevalent concept in Whitehall of 'lilly-padding' often also termed 'landing pads'. This concept says that to avoid failure in negotiations, it is necessary to know, before you commence negotiating, what your counter-part will agree to. If you can map those things that your counter-part is likely to accept or agree to, you can ensure that your own demands 'land' within that area. The idea is that in this way you maximise the chances of success and minimise the risk of failure. A crucial element in the concept is how success and failure are defined by Whitehall. They are in fact defined by the degree of political embarrassment that does, or does not, result. They are defined by the the degree of political damage, not by national benefit. So, if a minister or government is embarrassed by the outcome, the negotiations have failed, if there is no political fallout or embarrassment, they have succeeded.

The first stage in the 'Lilly-padding process, therefore, is to enter into discussions with your counter-part to explore their position and map the 'pad' that you want to land on. The second is to frame your objectives accordingly.

It should be obvious to the reader what the drawback of this approach is.

The drawback is that your counter-part frames your objectives. Your objectives are designed to meet with their agreement, rather than to further or secure your own interests.

This shockingly flawed approach to negotiating unsurprisingly met with no success. EU negotiators responded to the initial 'landing pad' exploration by junior UK 'negotiators' by saying, "It is you, the UK that is leaving and wants a agreement. You tell us what you want and then we can tell you whether we agree, disagree or might agree with some alteration." The UK was entirely unprepared for that entirely reasonable response but had no alternative approach.

Even three years later it seemed that the government had still not learned that its negotiating method was utterly useless. Amber Rudd, former Home Secretary and Work and Pensions Secretary, in her resignation from Prime Minister Johnson's cabinet and the Conservative party in the summer of 2019 - nearly three years after Article 50 notice was triggered - cited, amongst several reasons for her departure, that there were "no landing pads" in relation to the Johnson government's negotiations with the EU. Even then she was framing the negotiations in those terms.

The fact that our 'negotiators' ere unable to map 'landing pads' meant that the government was unable to define what it wanted to ask for and was, therefore, unable to define its negotiating objectives or strategy. This is why publication of the so called 'position papers' was delayed and why, when they were eventually published, they were no more than vague, airy-fairy lists of what would be nice to have. The government was fearful of stating clear objectives that the EU would reject as this may be viewed by the UK media and people as failure. Indeed this flawed mindset ran even deeper. Staff were forbidden to undertake detailed analysis or formulate policy proposals in case these were to leak and cause political embarrassment. This was a cowardly government, comprised of cowardly politicians.

The third point is that, whilst hoping for success in obtaining a beneficial agreement with the EU, the government failed utterly to initiate contingency planning for a 'no deal' scenario until far too late. Preparations for such an eventuality were virtually non-existent by the expiry of the Article 50 two year notice period on 29th March 2019.

The Chancellor of the Exchequer, Philip Hammond reportedly blocked any attempt to initiate meaningful planning and preparation and Theresa May, the Prime Minister, failed to over-rule him and ensure that it was done. The rationale was that if the government were to be seen to plan for risks they may be criticised for expecting failure.

It is important to recognise that this is not an isolated example of political risk aversion. The lack of moral and political courage is endemic in the corridors of Whitehall. I have myself experienced this attitude in Whitehall, in relation to the Ukrainian crisis in 2014. Politicians and civil servants alike were fearful of planning for any possible escalation of the conflict in case the Russians got to hear of it and it damaged UK/Russian relations further. So, had that conflict escalated, the UK would have been behind the loop and at a severe disadvantage. Likewise, for different but similar reasons, the Blair government ignored the persistent violation of ceasefire agreements in Kosovo and Macedonia between 1998 and 2002 leading to punitive actions against the governments concerned and a failure to address root causes. This is why those conflicts and associated instability still dominate Balkan affairs.

The persistent failure to recognise the vital need for contingency planning is an example of incompetence of the first degree within government. Failure to undertake scenario based contingency planning is nothing short of extreme negligence. After the EU referendum, there was a distinct failure of leadership and knowledge in the cabinet as to what should be done, together with an institutionally compromised civil service. These flaws and their causes must be addressed so that they do not re-appear as, I believe they are likely to, following the UK's eventual departure from the EU and during the subsequent period of transition.

Because she was being subjected to increasing press criticism that talks with the EU were getting nowhere - which, because of the landing pad approach they were not - Prime Minister Theresa May took the extraordinarily weak step of offering to pay the EU a £39bn 'divorce payment'. This was, in reality, nothing more than a bribe to persuade Brussels to move to 'Phase Two' of the Brexit talks i.e. talks about future trade. The idea was that this, in turn, would enable the Prime Minister to present supposed 'progress'. Publicity of this fact was very smoothly avoided and it was presented as the UK's obligation and implied that it was separate from the overall context of ongoing talks. It was not. The deception worked.

When Brussels accepted the bribe and agreed to move to Phase Two, the BBC ran the headline *"Breakthrough deal paves way for future trade talks"* and the Daily Express ran the front page headline *"PM Gets Deal!"*.

The reality is that the Prime Minister bluffed the nation. She gave away £39bn of taxpayer's money so that she could cover up for her failure to get anywhere in the talks and lessen the media and political pressure on her government.

£39bn was committed and yet there was no actual progress. This was a political deception. Somehow, the media and the British people have forgotten entirely the cir

Another appalling blunder committed by the Prime Minister, her government and civil servants was to accept that the UK had responsibility for finding a solution to the implications of Brexit for the border between Northern Ireland and the Republic.

When EU negotiators told Theresa May that the UK leaving the Single Market and Customs Union would mean that there would have to be a 'hard' border between north and south; when they told her that the UK must take responsibility and come up with a solution, it seems she panicked.

She had a choice. Either she accepted the UK's responsibility for finding a solution, or she sent the ball straight back into the EU's court, which is what she should have done. Unfortunately, she chose the former course. She lacked the nous to counter the EU position.

There are two crucial facts to consider:

1. The UK was exercising its legal right to leave the European Union.

2. The reason that Brussels said there must be physical border controls on the border was not simply that the UK was leaving the EU, but that there is a complex mix of EU treaties, laws, regulations and mandates that require physical controls on the EU's external borders.

The Northern Ireland Backstop element of Theresa May's EU Withdrawal Agreement was designed not to prevent a problem for the UK, but to avoid otherwise inevitable legal problems *for the European Union* when the UK leaves.

As the issue lies with legal requirements placed on the EU by its own legislation - not in legal obligations placed on the UK - the origin of the problem lies not with Brexit, but with EU legislation.

Of course, the UK cannot possibly change EU legislation and it is therefore impossible for the UK to solve the problem. Given that situation, any agreement by the UK to accept responsibility for finding a solution is crazy, cannot be met and, as a consequence, would mean that the UK would remain tied to the EU if the Backstop were to be accepted. Thankfully, Boris Johnson was Abe to remove the Backstop

The stated UK position should be, and must always be, that the treaties, laws, regulations and mandates of the EU become a matter for the EU alone, not for the UK.

The EU's legal requirement that there must be physical controls on its external borders is not the UK's business post-Brexit.

The majority of border control requirements, and therefore the problem, has its origins in EU legislation, thus it is for the EU to solve, not the UK.

That is not to say that we, in the UK, should not discuss the issue with the EU and do what we can assist in the design and application of a solution. We have an intrinsic interest in good cross border relations and cooperation with the EU and with the Irish Republic, and we must be constructive and helpful. It would, however, be stupid for any future prime minister to do as Theresa May did and accept responsibility for a problem that is not of our making, has its origins in legislation that we do not control and is not in our gift to solve.

Theresa May and her civil servants lacked the knowledge, courage and the clear objectives necessary to guide them in responding to the EU in the correct way over the Irish border. The issues of leadership, confidence, knowledge, strategic acumen and clarity of purpose are recurring themes, are they not?

Concern that Irish Republicans could exploit the presence of physical controls to raise tensions and the potential implications for the Good Friday Agreement added to the government's uncertainty. May seems to have panicked, hesitated and all too rapidly accepted responsibility for finding a solution. In doing so, she and her team dug themselves and the country into a very deep hole in the form of the Northern Irish Backstop. It is a hole that the UK will never be able to climb out of entirely. It was an unforgivable error of the first degree the shadow of which will cloud progress for many years. It was an error born of the incompetence and unsuitability of too many of the people we elect to Parliament.

Let's be clear, and I make no apology for banging away at this, the Backstop associated with Theresa May's Withdrawal Agreement if it had ever been implemented, could not have been removed unless a legal solution were found – a legal solution that, as I've pointed out, the UK has not control over and could not influence. The inescapable conclusion is that if the Withdrawal Agreement and the Northern Ireland Backstop had been or, at some point in the future, were to be agreed to and implemented, the UK could never gain full independence from the European Union. We would leave the EU institutions – European Council, European Parliament etc – but would never be free to leave the EU's legal and regulatory frameworks without losing Northern Ireland by aligning it with the Irish Republic. This would mean ending Northern Ireland's inclusion in the Customs Territory of the UK, something that would be unacceptable to Unionists and, if any government considers that option for a moment, they would rapidly realise that it would pose far more of a threat to stability and peace on the island of Ireland than physical controls.

But that is not all.

Scandalously, Theresa May's Conservative government betrayed the country in other ways.

Behind the scenes, Theresa May and her civil servants offered to give away the family silver and many of the assets that we will need to help build a confident, strong society and economy post-Brexit.

They made a diplomatic commitment to participate in a level of defence integration that would have linked our defence policies to those of the EU post-Brexit. This includes tying us into EU defence procurement regimes that may well see us being unable to guarantee that UK ships, tanks and aircraft can be built in the UK if we want them to be. Furthermore, even after Brexit, it appears the UK taxpayer may have been required to pay into the European Defence Fund (in effect an EU defence budget).

May also agreed so to continue to coordinate our foreign policy with that of the EU, as we presently do under Article 34 of the Lisbon Treaty. As a result, we would not have regained full independence of our foreign policy post-Brexit.

An area in which the UK leads the world is that of satellite research, technology and production. The Conservative government under May agreed that priorities, policies and investment relating to our satellite research and production industry would be aligned with those set by the European Commission.

Many politicians, ministers and MPs are open about their wish to see us remain within the framework of the EU Customs Union. Indeed, that is the official policy of the Labour Party, and, no doubt, such calls will continue even after the UK has left. However, such a policy would see our trade laws, negotiations, agreements and deals continue to be placed firmly under the influence of the European Union. In practice, if these people were to get their way and any government were to go along with it, even after Brexit, the UK will be unable to conclude its own deals with the rest of the world and many of our tariffs and border controls will be dictated by those of the EU. Disputes would be decided in EU courts, not our own.

How can we possibly become a confident, globally outward looking trading nation if our foreign, trade and defence policies are all subordinate, to any degree, to those of the EU? The answer is that we cannot.

The Withdrawal Agreement, as negotiated by the May government, even without the so called Backstop and Political Declaration, was not a Brexit agreement, it was a draft treaty with the European Union that would have ceded UK sovereignty and would have bound us for decades to EU legislation and policies. With then Backstop, it could have been for generations. It was a treaty that would have handicapped the UK's growth and prosperity for decades, post-Brexit.

Simply proposing such a restriction on our independence was a betrayal of the nation and the 2016 referendum result. Proposing it without making a concerted and significant attempt to explain the small print to the public was worse than a betrayal; it was fraud; it was a rejection of the principles of transparency, accountability and therefore democracy. It demonstrated an arrogance that should be utterly unacceptable in British politics. Without transparency, there can be no democracy and without democracy, there is no accountability.

The May government's European Union (Withdrawal) Act 2018 was a betrayal brought about by lack of leadership, vision, strategic grasp, confidence, integrity, knowledge and ability. Even as a draft, it demonstrated many of the all too common shortcomings amongst our national politicians.

Thankfully, primary as a result of the pressure exerted by the Brexit Party and its success in the 2019 EU Parliamentary Election, Boris Johnson became Prime Minister and was able to negotiate a number of amendments to the Withdrawal Agreement and the removal of the Backstop which, together, have made the Agreement one that could indeed deliver Independence in law, government and public administration. Whether or not it does, given that much of the detail has been left for the Transition Period, and that the government may yet drop, time will tell.

12

PSEUDO-SOCIAL LIBERALISM

Margret Thatcher, Tony Blair and David Cameron, not forgetting that the latter was influenced by Nick Clegg, in chasing middle ground voters, reduced the breadth of British politics as they moved their parties to the centre. This was an evolution aimed, largely successfully, at grabbing the votes of the new middle class, a group that has increasingly adopted the tenets of social liberalism.

Proper social liberalism emphasises the rights and autonomy of the individual. Individual rights and autonomy are seen as at harmony with the common good of society. Social liberal politicians prioritise rights, poverty, healthcare, education and the environment in their policies and claim to occupy a centrist, reasonable, compromising, intellectual and moderate position in politics. So far, so good.

The thing is that in the present day world almost all mainstream politicians claim this position. There are Labour, Conservative, Liberal Democrat, Green, Brexit Party and UKIP and other party politicians and members who claim to be social liberals. It is not a claim made only by members of the Liberal and Social Democrats.

Social Liberalism is an attractive position for politicians to claim because, incorrectly but by implication, the alternative is to be identified as less reasonable, compromising, intellectual and moderate, perhaps even extreme. It is a politically advantageous position to claim, whatever one's actual politics are.

I call politicians who deceptively adopt the cloak of social liberal respectability, so that they can obtain electoral support and deflect criticism, as 'pseudo-social liberals'. Whilst actually focusing on what are generally Marxist, socialist or leftist values, often extreme in character, they mask themselves with a 'social liberal' identity. In reality are far from liberal. In reality they reject all positions and opinions that differ from their own in a very illiberal, undemocratic way.

I talk about liberal extremism and the flawed left/right spectrum concept at length in Chapter 19, where I also propose an alternative, radial view of politics.

The unfortunate reality is that the middle ground of British society has become increasingly self-interested, partly because the pressures of life leave little time or attention for anything else. That is understandable and I do not criticise them for that. However, as stated, those of the supposed middle ground who have become pseudo-social liberals tend to reject opinions other than their own. In particular they reject and seek to alienate those that challenge their world view. Many of them measure effective politics by whether their personal wealth, assets and opportunities are growing. Any opinion or argument that challenges them, or proposes change, is considered a threat to their comfortable life by these people and they attempt to suppress the expression of such ideas. They sometimes do so by employing intimidation and/or the arguments of political correctness and equal representation.

Pseudo-social liberals have adopted the cloak of social liberalism to present themselves as morally correct 'do-gooders' whereas they are in fact rather privileged, increasingly self-indulgent, relatively privileged - albeit that they don't see themselves as such - and out of touch with broader society. They want a say in everything but are generally disinterested in the nitty gritty of things. They don't care about the inconvenient details or want to hear about problems and obstacles to be overcome and they dismiss the reality of international and national affairs. They are mostly opposed to Brexit because they see only financial and social risk for themselves. They are disinterested in potential opportunities for the nation as a whole.

Many members of this 'elite', those within the group but of a socialist left tendency, also reject the reality that there are differences in the innate skills, attributes, abilities, strengths and weaknesses that shape every human being. They seek to flatten society, moderate excellence and demand that they should have entirely equal access to everything regardless of ability or merit or ability. They demand that everybody adheres to social liberalism and they reject everything else. They reject hierarchy, defer to nobody and want to see government, business and society achieve a flat structure. They call for everyone to have equal opportunities, fair enough, but they also demand the right to express themselves and influence and shape events, regardless of their abilities, strengths and weaknesses. In reality, what they want is to be able to have a say in everything, whilst claiming the moral authority to reject the right of those who differ in opinion to have the same right.

I suspect that the truth is that leftist pseudo-social liberals are united by their insecurity. They seek to enhance their self-esteem and do so by highlighting how unfair life and society is. This in turn engenders a degree of bitterness and many appear to have quite a chip on the shoulder. They are unable to accept the fact that they may not be best suited to everything or, in some cases, anything. They are unable to accept that perhaps others do have experience and abilities in some areas that they do not; they are often unable to accept responsibility for themselves and their own life choices. They blame others yet reject the concepts of leadership and authoritative institutions that are required to direct and execute the affairs of state efficiently, unless they have a role in them.

Other members of this pseudo-social 'elite - for that is truly how some of them think of themselves - in particular those of a more Thatcherite through to New Labour tendency, see the purpose and measure of politics as being to open the doors of personal affluence and often influence and, as I have said, measure good politics by what they will gain personally rather than how society or the nation as a whole might benefit.

What both the socialist and Thatcherite/Blairite elements within the pseudo-social liberal group share is their responsibility for, and support of, a massive rise in 'political correctness' and 'identity politics'.

That rise has occurred because, by employing the arguments of political correctness and identity politics they obtain the means to, however artificially, justify the rejection of views, perceptions and opinions that differ from their own, or that challenge their comfortable, convenient even, assumptions about life. They would rather deny the validity of an argument they are uncomfortable with, and reject it out of hand, rather than consider and reflect upon it first.

As the pseudo-social liberal elite has grown and not been confronted, so has the often vicious, abusive rejection of broader opinions. The impact has been exponential as this 'elite' and its views, along with its bias, has permeated parliament, the civil service, media, national politics, education, the police and the judiciary.

Education is perhaps the key and I would posit that when the Labour Party introduced tuition fees in 1998 the impact was far reaching.

Students have always rebelled or pushed up against authority. We expect it of young people as they establish themselves and their ideas as independent, free-thinking members of society. The majority of students are very decent people, with a sense of responsibility and instinctively explore the world and society. This is an important time as they form the opinions that shape their future. However, this very dynamic means that universities have always provided a recruiting ground for militant socialism and those students with a tendency towards abusive anti-establishment behaviour are often encouraged by subversive elements amongst teaching staff.

Prior to 1998 and the introduction of tuition fees, there existed a concept that created a moral but moderate constraint on excessive rebelliousness (I should point out here that I believe everyone should have a little bit of the rebel in them). The concept was that those who receive benefits, in this case a state funded education, have no right to be truculent or demanding. The established belief was that those who pay should be entitled to make the rules. After

1998, that all changed. Not only was the cost of education unfairly passed to students, but, by removing the moral obligation on the part of students to be grateful to the state for providing for their education, the Labour Party created a breeding ground for left-wing, anti-social and pseudo-social liberal politics.

Frustration on both the left and the right of politics has grown as this pseudo-social liberal 'elite' has rejected and suppressed views at variance to their own, isolating and undermining the contribution of others. People like Owen Jones claim to embrace diversity when, in fact, through their rejection of broader opinions, they actively attempt to suppress it. When they are pushed, we find them withdrawing into defensive arguments in support of cultural and ethnic diversity, whilst actually continuing to act to suppress diversity of thought and opinion. This, combined with the financial stresses born out of austerity, the reduction in public services and lack of public investment in the regions, fuelled and continues to fuel growing frustration and extremism on the right.

Legitimate expression of concerns over the rapid changes experienced by communities, the management of immigration, the rise in violent crime or the encouragement of primary school pupils to explore their gender is now worryingly condemned as extreme.

To express concern at society's limited ability to absorb and support increasing numbers of immigrants is labelled as 'racist'.

Those who quite legitimately supported the UK's exit from the European Union were labelled xenophobic little Englanders.

Debate concerning issues of the day are laced with insults and abuse lacking in genuine political argument.

Social media platforms have a great deal to answer for by allowing anonymity. That anonymity enables individuals to smear and abuse others online, without exposing themselves to accountability.

But social media is not the cause, it is a medium. The cause is a growing acceptance that it's alright to employ abuse and insults to deter or discredit the expression of views, ideas and opinions you disagree with. Anonymity facilitates online bullying, intimidation and oppression. This behaviour is a product of extreme pseudo-social liberals and their condemnation of everyone truly liberal. Now there is a mind-twister that illustrates the contortions that British politics are experiencing.

More moderate people are deterred from standing up against this assault of pseudo-social liberalism and keep their heads down, out of the line of fire. They try to ignore it at best, appease it at worst.

Equal representation, which I talk about more in Chapter 17, has exacerbated the problem. It has smothered equal opportunities and has encouraged racial, cultural and religious prejudice, causing a rise in tension, abuse and violence along ethnic, cultural, gender and sexual orientation lines.

The frustration bred out the rejectionist attitude of the centre ground, middle-class, liberal elite is one of the reasons for the rise of both left and right wing extremism, the rise of Momentum has both fed it and fed off it whilst the significant shift to the right of UKIP and other groups is in reaction to it. The left and right of politics are pushing back against each other, demanding the right to express themselves and in doing so have developed an ugly character that increasingly relishes confrontation and feeds polarisation.

I say again, expressing concerns regarding the manner in which we manage our borders, migration and the integration of immigrants into British society does not necessarily make a person racist. Expressing worries that our judicial system is overly lenient and our policing politicised or too politically correct is not authoritarian. Worrying about the wisdom of encouraging primary school pupils to explore their gender is not transphobic. Advocating the UK's full independence from the EU in all areas of law, government and public administration does not make a person a xenophobe, racist or a 'little Englander'.

We, as a society, allow the rejection of the expression of legitimate concerns at our peril. To suppress the expression of opinions is to limit freedom of speech, is illiberal, undemocratic and encourages the growth of a passion and extremism that in turn rejects moderate views thereby creating a vicious circle.

Pseudo-social liberals and their self-righteous condemnation of the opinions and concerns of others, are to blame for this increasingly nasty, bitter, socially divisive cycle of cause and effect that they continue to be the catalyst for.

I said in a previous chapter that much of our strength, as a nation, is that we are generally, by both tradition and custom, profoundly compassionate and nonconformist. The pseudo-social liberal movement severely threatens that character. It is intrinsically lacking in sincere compassion and demands conformity with its own world-view. It demands the very conformity that it claims to reject.

We, as a society must become more open to the expression of concerns, views and ideas. Yes, even those we do not like or agree with. We must resist the bullies who seek to silence us, or insult and abuse us, if when we express disagreement. And, if we do not agree with someone else, we must counter with reasoned debate and persuasive argument, not with blind rejection or insults.

We are, as a society, gradually losing the ability to discuss and debate issues in a civilised, tolerant and respectful manner. The arts of rhetoric and debate are no longer taught in our schools, but should be reintroduced.

Moreover, and importantly, the vast but silent majority of people are reasonable and worried by the the slide of society into intolerance. I would say to them that we must all find the courage to oppose suppression. We should stand up to it debate opinions that we disagree with, rather than shy away from doing so for fear of abuse. We must not remain silent and by doing so allow ourselves to be oppressed. We are the people and the nation belongs to us.

13

WESTMINSTER'S VILLAGE IDIOTS

IT'S A PEOPLE PROBLEM

At times of great moment or crisis in the history of our islands, the one thing that has always emerged is leadership. So, why is it that now, when leadership and direction are so badly needed to navigate the country through Brexit and beyond, there is no one to provide it? No leader has emerged who the nation as a whole has confidence in.

People are crying out for inspiration and a vision behind which the nation can unite in a common effort to revive a sense of purpose and pride.

Where is a politician able to bring back a feeling of confidence, optimism, prosperity and security in being British and make it sustainable; a leader with strategic vision, bold enough to deal sensibly with immigration, take on lawlessness, remove much of nightmarishly complicated tax burden, distribute investment around the country based on need rather than where a particular political party's support base or targeted voters lie; leadership that serves by leading and inspiring rather than by chasing votes.

The bitter truth is that there is no such leadership in

Westminster, or amongst our MPs. For perhaps the first time in centuries, our parliament has failed to produce one person who stands out as being up to the task. As I have said repeatedly:

"The risks associated with Brexit do not lie in leaving the European Union, but in having a government and parliament so negligent and incompetent as to be unable to manage the process".

Unfortunately, I have been proven correct. Our politicians, as a whole, are not up to the task.

To lead and govern effectively means possessing vision the intellect to be able to conceive distant objectives, inspire, motivate, prioritise and unify efforts; to work steadily with drive and determination towards those objects whilst retaining the fleetness of foot required to address the unforeseen, the immediate and the urgent.

With few exceptions, parliamentarians of recent years have been lacking in such traits. They have been egotistical, out of touch, ill-informed and often pretty dim and dull career politicians incapable of making anything but routine decisions in a 'steady as she goes' environment.

Brexit has revealed the appalling state of British politics in general and the failings of our parliamentarians in particular.

The excruciatingly poor performance of many of our MPs, their propensity for soundbite politics and belief that parliament and not the people is sovereign, have served only to undermine confidence in British politics to such an extent that ever more people are agitating for a total reform of our system.

This has created opportunities for increasingly 'populistic' politicians, who offer no plan or methodology, who gathering cult-like support by promising to sweep aside centuries of lessons learned, political evolution and institutions. They offer no credible policies but offer the word; they mobilise people by appealing to the emotive side of human nature; those things that arouse critical rather than inspirational passion. This is dangerous.

The reality is that people are easily roused to passion, excitement and action by an idea, concept or principle. Such vaguely defined concepts as sovereignty, freedom, liberty, independence are examples of causes for which people will lay down their lives.

People so roused are not interested in, or concerned by, the practicalities of delivering government. They are bored by such things. They demand action not words, they want to hear no excuses, they are not prepared to accept obstacles. They expect all challenges to be swept aside.

To be able to mobilise and harness public opinion and passion behind a vision, with the ability to manage and direct that passion towards attaining great but realistic things; towards building a more confident, optimistic, prosperous nation; to be able to strengthen belief in our system, rather than undermine our society, our government and its ability to serve the people, is a great thing.

Mobilising the passion of large numbers of people without having a coherent vision and plan for achieving great things, without being able to harness and manage that passion and activism once unleashed, without setting realistic expectations, that is the hight of political irresponsibility.

Even when able to manage such a movement, there is a responsibility placed upon its leaders to abide with the conventions of our unwritten constitution and to respect and protect our constitutional institutions, if not the people within them. A failure to do so, whilst at the head of a mobilised and passionate movement, is to create a revolutionary mood that the UK does not want or need.

The fundamental truth is that, in every case, even when decisions may be taken rapidly, change takes time to plan and implement and is rarely immediate. Change, without exception, creates a degree of uncertainty and instability that must be managed. To sweep aside institutions, alter our constitutional system or even promise to do such things in a short period so as to excite and exploit the passion of people and grab polling numbers on the back of populistic support is irresponsible.

Our politicians, whether in parliament or not, must be intelligent enough, mature enough and sufficiently worldly wise to understand this and the importance of mobilising passion and political emotions only when they can lead them toward great and beneficial ends.

It is also crucial to understand and appreciate the value of the fact that there are two parts to government. There are those parts that give it resilience, stability, rules and resources and there are those that give it flexibility, adaptability, impact and efficiency. As Water Baghot, the 19th century constitutionalist who authored 'The English Constitution', observed, the "dignified" parts of government - what I call its institutions - raise the army and provide it with resources, they do not win the battles. Anyone who seeks to sweep aside those institutions, or dignified parts, or promises wholesale reform without a thorough understanding of the second and third order effects, is playing with fire.

In searching for where the problems lie, and where to apply change, it is vital to recognise that it is not our constitutional structure or its institutions that are flawed, although some reforms are desperately needed, it is the men and women who staff them and the system that selects them that are at fault.

We do not need to sweep aside the House of Lords or remove its powers. We need to radically alter the manner in which Peers are selected to sit in that place.

It is not the two party system that needs to be overturned – there is no such thing as the 'two party system' in any case – but the first past the post electoral system that must be changed. 'First past the post' reduces effective democratic representation and allows just two parties to dominate political life in the UK. Proportional representation must be introduced as a matter of urgency.

By enabling greater representation through the presence of smaller parties in the House of Commons, proportional representation would provide the opportunity for the public and politicians alike to observe, hear and consider the different methods, ideas and solutions of those parties. For example, some may emerge with selection processes that produce competent political candidates, people who do possess real leadership ability. This in turn would encourage a positive change in the character of the politics of this country generally.

To attempt to implement such irresponsible, headline grabbing and populistic ideas as "abolishing the House of Lords", as some politicians have advocated, without having given serious thought as to how to implement those changes, to what beneficial end and without understanding the implications, would be to invite unforeseen and possibly catastrophic results for our country's good governance.

Simply calling for such things, only to enhance populistic support and polling figures, without making any coherent proposals, is highly irresponsible. As I have already said, but it bears saying again, such calls ignore the reality that the problems in our political system do not lie with our institutions, but with the people who lead them, govern them and populate them, along with the procedures they employ.

Reform is always required, to ensure adaptation to an ever evolving social, economic and political environment and set of needs, but politically opportunistic and wholesale destruction is not a sound approach and must be resisted.

Sweeping aside institutions or the 'dignified' parts of government will not work. Doing so would fail to solve any of the problems facing society and the nation, however, it would risk fundamentally weakening our national administration and its ability to address and manage those problems. Furthermore, rather like devolution, once done, such things cannot be undone and I simply do not trust our national politicians to have the strategic acumen to assess and manage the consequences of such a move properly.

Our constitutional structures took many centuries to build and evolve and have proved their worth repeatedly in times of national crisis. They are by character dependable and they provide steadiness, depth and resilience for the nation. They also protect it from the abuses or excesses of overly ambitious, authoritarian or extreme governments. Perhaps they may be disassembled in months, but they could then never again be put back.

Sweeping away institutions is not needed or helpful and is inherently dangerous. The great majority of challenges we are experiencing with government and today's political system are people related, not due to flaws in our institutional structures. We must resist calls to break the fundamental building blocks of our system whilst failing to address the actual problem.

There is a significant obstacle to addressing the people problems of Westminster and Whitehall. That obstacle is that it is far easier to blame institutions for our difficulties and failings than it is to blame people. It is an easy option. It is easier to blame a thing than a person as the 'thing' will not defend itself in the same way, and a 'thing' is not a friend, colleague or ally and did not go to the same school or work in the same legal firm.

Blaming an institution also presents a lot more easily. Highlighting the shortfalls of the House of Lords, the civil service or foreign aid is a great deal more straight forward than explaining why and how to reform the civil service, the way in which political parties select candidates or the intricacies of foreign aid. It is easier for lazy politicians and it is easier for an electorate that has a very limited attention span.

Blame requires less explanation and arouses greater passion than solutions. Human beings are by nature and by biology orientated to respond with energy to perceived threats and problems. That is why negative, blame culture politics that point the finger at something as a problem, attract a passionate following.

The EU, as a thing, is blamed for so many ills. Brexiteers, as a group (thing), are blamed for threatening the prosperity of the UK.

The Lords' predominantly 'remain' position on Brexit caused great ire amongst Brexiteers. Subsequently there have been calls, led by Nigel Farage, for the abolishion of the House of Lords. But it is not the House of Lords, as an institution, that is the issue. It is the members of the House of Lords that Farage holds truck with.

In contrast, discussion about solutions tends to be practical rather than emotive, boring rather than exciting, dull rather than impassioning.

People, not institutions are the issue. So let me be boring for a moment and talk about the people.

The Brexit debate in parliament exposed beyond denial that many MPs held and perhaps still do hold the electorate in deep contempt. The country was told by its Prime Minister at the time, David Cameron, that the referendum vote in 2016 was *"a once in a life-time decision"*; that *"whatever you decide will be implemented"* yet, three years later, the country found itself no closer to leaving the European Union than it was on the 24th June 2016.

Campaigners, MPs and some former Prime Ministers said, and still say, *"but the people didn't know what they were voting for"* and *"Brexit will do immense damage"*. Such assertions are absolute tosh, nobody knows with absolute certainty what the long term economic outcome will be. However, even if such prophecies of doom were proven to be correct at some point in the future, 'project fear' assertions were made very clearly and publicly by the government before the referendum and yet, despite that, 17.4 million people still voted to leave. Their motive was not economic. The assertion of the right to self-determination was at the centre of the referendum result.

As for the repeated and impassioned calls for a second referendum, or 'people's vote', who voted last time, if not the people?

In order to evade the argument that a second referendum would be a dangerous precedent, potentially leading to calls for referenda to confirm any democratic vote - including general elections - politicians and campaigners who called for a second referendum argued that it should not be a repeat of the question whether or not to leave the EU. Rather, they argued that such a 'people's vote' should be on the acceptance or otherwise of a proposed deal between the UK and the EU.

Let's consider that for a moment.

Theresa May's proposed Withdrawal Agreement 'deal' was 599 pages long. Now, with all due respect to the British electorate, did Remain politicians and campaigners really expect voters to read, understand and make a judgement as to the efficacy of all the complex issues covered in all 599 pages of such a document?

If that really was or indeed is the expectation, it would be very hard to take any such campaigner seriously.

I would argue that expecting the average voter to have the time, interest and inclination to read, inwardly digest, research and understand every one of the 599 pages would is so demonstrative of derangement and disconnection with real world as to make those people arguing such a thing unfit to hold any position of responsibility.

If campaigners for a 'people's vote' on such a question really understood that the electorate cannot be expected to undertake such deep research and analysis, then clearly, their stated intention of seeking to ensure that the electorate was provided with a chance to make an informed decision was entirely false.

That being the case, it becomes obvious that such campaigners were motivated by a desire to prevent the UK's departure from the EU; a desire to overturn or reverse the result of the referendum held on 23rd June 2016 before it could be implemented. Such people cock a snoot at democracy, hold the electorate in contempt and have no place in a democratic system such as ours.

This display of contempt for our democracy is disturbing and deeply harmful. It undermines public belief in our politicians and our political system and it provides ammunition for, and encouragement to those who seek a more extreme form of politics and government. It also provides grist for the mill of populism and those who utilise the politics of the crowd, making promises that they never expect to be in a position to have to implement. Politics without responsibility is the home of the snake oil salesman, cad (see Chapter 18) and extremist.

Furthermore, the fact that many of our politicians fail to comprehend the damage they are doing, demonstrates the scale of the gap in comprehension between society and its elected representatives. It also reveals their seriously worrying lack of altruistic intellect.

Elected politicians would do well to learn that we elect them to serve individually and collectively in the interests of the nation, not to indulge their own egos, interests, crusade or agenda.

What to do? How do we address the people problem?

The first step in working out what to do; how to tackle the appalling lack of leadership and vision within our political system, is to understand why it is that so many uninspiring individuals become political candidates and why it is that we then vote them into office. It is quite bizarre when you think about it.

Where did the rot begin? Rot is a gradual process. Does it commence with the conditions necessary for it to set in, or does it start with the first spores?

Well, let us start here....

The European Union has, by duplicating the political and administrative functions present in its member states, has usurped the customary requirement for our Parliament to function and cabinet to govern in anything but a steady, highly regulated environment. Strategies formulated by the EU and decisions made in Brussels, not in national capitals, have lead to weak and feeble politics and unimaginative, process driven administrations in the EU member states. As such, the legislatures of EU member states are no longer the breeding grounds of great leaders, of men and women with the capacity to inspire and govern with passion, determination and wisdom, that they once were.

An era of self-centred, self-interested, self-indulgent and materialistically minded politics was made possible by environment created by the European Union and given birth to, in the UK, by Thatcherism and New Labour.

The concept of New Labour, as promoted in the mid 1990s by Tony Blair, Peter Mandelson, Alistair Campbell and Gordon Brown moved Labour from its traditional, socialist, left wing politics - which had been weakened and made less attractive due to the demise of British manufacturing, the working class and Thatcher's focus on individual opportunities. Blair et al deliberately moved he Party to the centre-left in a largely successful attempt to grab the votes of the new middle class, a group emboldened by Thatcher and which increasingly interpreted effective politics as that which increased their own personal assets and opportunities; a group, the self-identifying members of which now adopt the cloak of social liberalism and do so in order to present themselves as 'do-gooders' when many are in fact simply self-indulgent.

David Cameron, a self-identifying economic and social

liberal, also moved the Conservative Party away from traditional conservatism and towards the centre, again chasing the vote of a growing middle class that identified with Blair. Cameron even took to dressing like him, dropping the jacket and tie, a habit he developed to bluff the voters that he was a man of the people. Cameron was from a broadly similar political mould to Blair, whose "profound understanding" he praised. He appealed to a Blairite generation that didn't appreciate of Gordon Brown's politics or, later, those of Jeremy Corbyn. Like Blair, Cameron offered growing opportunities to the middle class at the cost of the working class and the regions. However, he continued the Conservative libertarian economic model, accelerating the selling off and outsourcing of public services and utilities in a process established by Blair.

Thatcher, Blair and Cameron are, all three, responsible for the new, damaging self-centredness in politics, based around personal wealth and affected social liberalism. We can only speculate how things might have evolved had the emphasis instead been on confidence and optimism for all.

Their governments, and that of Brown, empowered the middle class and their social liberal politics. Those three Prime Ministers deliberately enabled what is sometimes referred to as the 'Liberal Elite', centre/centre left political class, to establish itself firmly in British politics and society. With it has come to a de facto suppression of views that, until the early 1990s had been perfectly acceptable as contributions to the national debate, but are now considered not to coincide with those of social liberals.

By the mid-1990s Tony Blair and 'New Labour' were broadening the appeal of the Labour Party by moving away from its socialist roots to increase its appeal to the political centre ground, middle class. Rather than being a party that said, "This is what we believe in. If you agree, vote for us" Labour, under Blair became a party that chased the vote. It abandoned the party's socialist background and principles and broadened its presentation according to what people wanted to hear. It chased votes, manipulated and encouraged materialistically minded, middle-class, centre left voters and imposed a united message on the members of its own parliamentary party - its MPs.

In moving away from its historical politics, it became difficult to say what New Labour stood for.

Blair also introduced the concept of all women female parliamentary candidate short-lists for the 1997 general election, a practice only found elsewhere in South America and South Korea. This so called 'affirmative action' rather than recognising and addressing the root causes behind fewer women applying to become candidates, exercises positive discrimination. In this way, Blair became responsible in large part for encouraging the deeply unhealthy and harmful growth of identity politics and equal representation, both of which have seriously harmed healthy progress towards ever more equal opportunities.

David Cameron learned from New Labour. As I've already pointed out, he was an open admirer of Blair and replicated much of Blair's admittedly successful - in terms of votes - approach. The Conservatives, under Cameron, employed New Labour's strategy against it, by also moving towards the centre.

The Blair/Cameron strategy of occupying and consolidating the centre ground of British politics had three implications.

Firstly, for the two parties to appeal to the centre they, of course, had also to move their parliamentary parties to the centre ground. This meant that their parliamentary candidates had to be drawn from the social liberal centre audience. Labour and Conservative parties had to impose a united message on the members of their parliamentary party to curb more passionate socialist or conservative views. Candidates and elected politicians were, and are, expected to 'tow the party line' and do as they are told perhaps more so than at any other time in history. The party whips in parliament have been given sweeping powers to keep MPs from straying too far from their party's official thinking. Breaking ranks was, and is, punishable.

It can rightly be argued that party discipline has always been necessary. The change, however, is that in the past, politicians were loyal to the principles or ideology of their respective parties but, as those principles have been abandoned by the the struggle for the middle ground vote, party cohesion has broken down. Policies are now, generally, opportunistic vote grabbers rather than principles or ideologically based. Hence discipline is required to force MPs to vote in a particular way and independently thinking politicians are considered difficult by their party management.

This closing down of open thinking and internal debate within parties has, in turn, led to the isolation and exclusion of visionary leadership material; the sidelining of imaginative political characters and thinkers. It has led to a significant increase in young politicians who are compliant but who possess little life experience to give them depth. The new breed of politician is generally grateful to their party for the chance given to them and, as such, are more loyal and compliant. The candidates and elected members of the Brexit Party are no different and have been selected for much the same reasons as those of other parties; for loyalty and ability to enable the 'army' to field troops, rather than for their effectiveness. Very few modern politicians and MPs are the strategic or independent thinkers, problem solvers and influencers that national politics, the government and the nation require.

Only a political party united by a common belief amongst its members in a shared strategic vision and objectives, rather than simple adherence to, and compliance with an economic or political doctrine, will have any chance of developing the independent characters, thinkers, problem solvers and influencers - the leaders - we need.

The move to attract the votes of the centre clearly and deliberately isolated those who have remained on the left and the right of politics.

It was the reaction of the socialist left to its abandonment by New Labour that fed the growth of Momentum and led to the election of Jeremy Corbyn as Labour Party leader.

It was the abandonment of traditional, patriotic conservatism by the Conservative Party under Cameron that led to the growth of the UK Independence Party and its attraction to the extreme right.

Those on the extremities of British politics are re-asserting themselves. However, this isn't simply British politics finding a new balance. The bitterness born of political isolation, combined with stresses caused by the May government's procrastination over Brexit, means that the process has become increasingly polarised, hostile and confrontational.

Another way of saying this is that the dominance of social liberal centre in politics since the 1990s and the de facto rejection of broader opinion have encouraged bitterness, resistance and extremism at both ends of the spectrum. Brexit then provided the battlefield and the delay in delivering it provided the adversaries with time to mobilise.

The social liberals of all parties have become the new ruling class, employing political correctness and identity politics to condemn the expression of opinions that challenge their own. Increasing numbers are rebelling at having their opinions and ideas written off.

I mentioned Identity Politics. This is the third worrying trend that gained traction during the Blair/Cameron era and is growing in influence. The topic is sufficiently significant and concerning that, I have dedicated Chapter 17 to it.

14

THE STRANGE DEATH OF LEADERSHIP

WHATEVER HAPPENED TO 'SERVE TO LEAD"?

Labour and the Conservatives have chased social liberal, middle ground votes, and pseudo-social liberals in all parties but particularly on the left of British politics, have attempted to shut out anything other than their brand of 'centrist' political opinion. This has led to the exclusion from mainstream national politics of dynamic political thinkers and characters with the knowledge, experience and ability to challenge conventional thought constructively for the greater good.

As the Labour and Conservative parties in the 90's and first years of the 21st century gathered ever more tightly around the privileged, middle class, centre ground, their leaders had to expend ever more effort reigning in the left and right wings of their parties. People with independent, imaginative, explorative and visionary minds that could be very useful in providing solutions or in responding to crises are difficult to manage and are unwanted in today's political parties. So, by default parties recruit ever greyer and uninspiring candidates from the middle ground for Westminster elections. Followers, not leaders.

This trend coincided with the growth, in the 1990s, of the view that 'leadership' was a directive, autocratic and outdated concept. The social liberals elitists do not appreciate being told what to do; they do not want anyone else to set the agenda; they rebel against authority.

To them, the term 'management' was and is considered a vastly more acceptable term than 'leadership' as it implies a more consultative, compromising and therefore, in their minds, more reasonable approach to running things.

Of course, there still have to be frameworks in the workplace, in business and life generally. These have traditionally and effectively been provided by a combination of leadership and management.

The role of leadership is to establish the vision, inspire and to set strategic objectives and direction. Management oversees the practical implementation of laws, regulations, systems and procedures that ensure things are done 'correctly' and provide the basis for training those who are to do them.

However, the discouragement of the term 'leadership' has led to a loss of strategic perspective, acumen and inspiration; to vagueness of vision, direction and unity of effort.

All efforts should be driven towards agreed and established goals in all walks of life, but lack of leadership, vision and the ability to inspire means this rarely happens.

The de facto rejection of the concept of 'leadership' in the 1990s and 2000s left, not unsurprisingly, a leadership void. This was and still is filled by rules, procedures, processes and managers. This, and the fact that managers rarely embrace change means that there has been a reduction in the opportunities for those people with vision, imagination and creativeness. The 'keepers of the processes' do not generally appreciate visionaries because visionaries want to change things. In a managed environment, they are disruptive and seen as difficult.

It is normal for people who are potential leaders or able to support the leadership effort directly, to be perceived by their bosses, consciously or otherwise, as a headache and potential threat to their authority. This is particularly the case of 'superiors', such as Blair and Cameron. I could name others; people with large egos who dislike sharing the limelight or who, like Theresa May, are themselves personally narrow, insecure and lacking the deep, rather than affected, self-confidence needed to work effectively with those of real genius.

As an aside, an interesting exception was the appointment by Prime Minister Boris Johnson, of Dominc Cummings - a prominent Leave campaign organiser - to the post of special adviser to the government. Like him or loathe him, Cummings is a very difficult character. Disliked by many and divisive in many ways, there is no doubting his political vision, sagacity, focus and problem solving skills. In appointing Cummings Johnson showed a rare (these days) degree of leadership and self-confidence.

So, up and coming leaders tend to be difficult and unwelcome. Winston Churchill must have been a nightmare to 'lead', precisely because he was himself leadership material. The Duke of Wellington, like Churchill, was considered by his mother to have been a "difficult child". Potential leaders may indeed be difficult, but they are necessary. We need them at least as much as we need managers, although we need fewer of them.

I would suggest that, in very general terms, in the context of government and public administration, politicians should be inspirational leaders, possessing strategic acumen setting objectives and overall direction. Civil servants should be the managers, advisers and problem solvers.

The upshot of all this is that the imaginative, expressive, decisive, often eccentric and generally difficult characters who could have been today's political leaders were, and continue to be, unable to make headway in mainstream politics. Parliament is full of grey, timid, unimaginative and indecisive men and women, many of whom take themselves very seriously but most of whom are not extraordinary in any way.

In the UK, unlike any other European state, all our ministers are drawn from the assembly - a good thing - so, it should not be any surprise that, when our MPs are generally of such low calibre, our cabinet is also comprised of equally uninspiring individuals.

Leadership is perhaps, above all, an attitude. Almost all politicians claim to hold our armed forces in high regard. I, therefore commend to them the motto of the Royal Military Academy Sandhurst: *"Serve to Lead"*. My sincere advice and request to them, and anyone considering a career in politics is:

"Should you be unable to grasp the meaning of the RMAS motto 'Serve to Lead', should you need it explaining or if disagree with the ethos behind it, you are not suited to politics. I'm afraid you are already or, if you are not, you will become part of the problem, not part of the solution".

Political parties should avoid selecting such people in the first place. They may be incredibly competent individuals, perhaps even liable, but they are not what the nation needs in the assembly or in the government.

15

THE CIVIL SERVICE & THE CASE FOR REFORM

ANONYMOUS PEOPLE, HIDDEN FROM VIEW AND BEYOND THE PUBLIC'S AWARENESS, HAVE IMPOSED SWATHES OF UNWANTED AND UNNECESSARY CHANGES THAT BENEFIT NOBODY

The most significant and challenging implication of Brexit is the requirement for comprehensive, strategic change in the civil service; complete, root and branch reform.

I have had the pleasure to work with many Whitehall civil servants over the past 20 or more years. I have invariably found them pleasant, intelligent and capable, hard working individuals. There is, however, a striking level of institutional conformity and a distinct lack of imagination within the service. The 'system' discourages lateral thinking.

Now, indulge me by picturing the following very much simplified, but accurate description of the decision-making process that has been in place whilst the UK has been a member state of the EU:

Along with the other 27 leaders of the European Union member states, our Prime Minister attends the European Council Heads of Government meetings in Brussels. These are held, irregularly, but around a dozen times a year.

The meetings are prepared mainly by EU civil servants in Brussels together with preparatory committees (PrepComs)

involving the 28 EU member state ambassadors. Essentially the content, background and briefings are provided by the EU. Policy decisions are drafted. 'PrepComs' approve them and they form the basis for the Heads of Government discussions.

The Heads of Government invariably have a great deal to get through during these gatherings. Discussions are intense and exhausting. The draft decisions are amended as required and, generally, approved.

Immediately on returning to London, the Prime Minister will normally convene a Cabinet meeting.

At that meeting he or she will brief ministers:

"As you know, I was in Brussels at the European Council. We discussed a), b), and c). We agreed 1), 2) and 3). So, we will need to follow up by doing x), y) and z)."

Ministers then return to their departments to brief their senior civil service team (who will almost certainly already have been briefed through their own chain):

"As you know, the PM was at the Council. The Council agreed 1), 2) and 3) and we, in the Department, have been asked to follow up by doing x)."

The departmental civil service then swings into action to implement the decision(s) made in Brussels.

That is the highest level of decision making and dissemination as it occurs in the EU.

Significantly, the European Commission has the authority to interpret these decisions, EU treaties and primary legislation and to issue further directives, policies, regulations and secondary legislation to support that interpretation.

These directives, policies, regulations and secondary legislation issued by the Commission are not generally subject to discussion with member states or EU Parliament, and are issued directly to the UK civil service, as instructions, as a matter of routine.

Now, here are the problems.

Firstly, given the comprehensive breadth and reach of EU decision making, policy, legislation and regulation, almost the entire UK civil service has been organised and is now fully orientated to implement and administer decisions and instructions from Brussels that cannot be appealed or revisited.

Therefore, the last thing that the 'system' wants is some clever junior or middle ranking civil servant who is going to stick their hand up and point out a problem or, suggest a better course of action. Why? Because going back through the system, all the way to the European Council or European Commission, to initiate a change, is virtually impossible. Challengers, however well meaning, constructive and correct, are not welcome in such an environment.

Secondly, the fact that a great deal of the policy and legal research, thinking, development and production is undertaken by EU civil servants makes the need for imaginative problem solvers and specialists within the Whitehall civil service somewhat redundant.

The reduced need for lateral thinkers and specialists, together with the requirements of having to implement and administer decisions made elsewhere, naturally influences internal management policy, processes and recruitment criteria.

The concept at present, is that civil servants should be 'generalists', not specialists. The policy of 'mobility', not without some merits, means that staff spend only 2-3 years in any one post and are, as a result, rarely able to accrue deep knowledge and a comprehensive grasp of their thematic or geographical area of work. For example, the Foreign and Commonwealth Office no longer recruits or trains linguists. It is public knowledge that the civil service lacked trade negotiators in the run up to Brexit. The UK hasn't had to negotiate a trade deal for decades, so it was, of course, reasonable not to employ or train such people. But we need them now.

This all means that new entrant civil servants have been selected for their process driven nature, rather than their imagination or problem solving skills. Additionally, over time and because of its predominantly implementation role, and the increasingly administrative bent of its staff, the management of the civil service has become exponentially process and procedure focused and has become less flexible and adaptable. This is one reason why the nation has become increasingly run by tick-box processes and no one appears able to simplify our mind-bogglingly complex tax system or the bureaucratic burdens that so distress ordinary people and businesses.

Now, and this is the point, the vulnerability created by prior dependence on the EU has been exposed by Brexit. Our national administrative capacity has been fundamentally weakened by our membership of the EU. The civil service has adapted to and become dependent upon its role of implementing EU decisions, policies, laws and regulations. It is not any longer structured or orientated towards strategy development, specialist knowledge, problem solving and initiative.

Institutionally, the civil service still struggles to grasp how the UK will manage itself without having the EU's framework within which those policies, laws and regulations are developed, decided and promulgated. That is why Brexit has met with such reluctance, some may say resistance, within the very institution on which the nation and its government rely in so many ways.

This is a problem of strategic, national importance.

As I said at the beginning of this chapter, going forward, the most significant, immediate and critical implication of Brexit is the absolute need for root and branch reform of the civil service. It is crucial to the nation's future success in every respect.

The previous approach of the civil service being staffed by 'generalists' (Jacks of all trades, masters of none), is no longer appropriate. Specialists and the mildly eccentric must be allowed back in. We will need analytical, problem solving characters who dislike and cannot work well when overly bound by processes and procedures, and who are often difficult to manage. They, their imagination and their energy are vital in supporting healthy and responsive government.

I have referred to the 'faceless people' a few times in this book. Let me turn to that topic now.

I pose the question again here, who are the unaccountable administrators who impose deep changes to our environment, culture and public services without us being told or consulted?

Of course, civil servants are led by politicians, but if we do not know which politicians made which decisions, how can they be accountable. For example, who was it who decided to outsource healthcare, prison and some policing services? Were we consulted? Were these changes described in detail in any party manifesto? Did we have the opportunity to vote for or against such major changes?

Who was it who decided to do away with many of our proud, historic, county regiments, sweeping away famous names and centuries of tradition: The Cheshires, The Devon

& Dorsets, The Hampshires, The Staffords, The Black Watch, The Royal Welch and many more? Was this a justifiable cost saving measure? No, it was not. Did it result in improved operational capacity or capability? No, it did not.

The majority of these regiments were amalgamated into large, new regiments without any significant savings. For example, The Devonshire and Dorset Regiment, Royal Gloucestershire Berkshire and Wiltshire Regiment, Royal Green Jackets, Light Infantry, Rifle Volunteers and elements of the Princess of Wales's Royal Regiment and London Regiment were simply 'rebadged' to form the 7 battalions of the new RIFLES Regiment.

Anonymous people, hidden from view and beyond the public's awareness, have imposed huge, unwanted and unnecessary changes that benefit nobody. Where does their authority come from, who gave it to them?

These people are unknown to us. There is little or no transparency into their world, or into the processes they apply. Without transparency, there can be no democracy and without democracy, there is no accountability.

Are we truly the oldest, or one of the oldest democracies in the world? Or are we no longer even a democracy?

Does this sound as though I am contradicting myself?

On the one hand, I have said we need to bring back the eccentric, imaginative problem solvers. On the other hand, I have suggested that too many decisions are being made without public support.

The solution to this apparent contradiction is far better and much more comprehensive planning on the part of political parties. Parties should be required not only to provide manifestos that persuade members of the electorate to vote for them, but that are concrete offers to the public. Manifestos should describe the work plan the party will pursue if it is elected, and parties should be held accountable for their adhearance to their work plans if indeed elected to office. Military reform, cuts to policing budgets, privatisation, or the sale of public assets, should all be described within that work plan or not be undertaken.

Presently, what happens is that the public is presented with manifestos that are simply "why you should vote for me/us" documents. They are not proposed work plans for parliament and government. They should be.

16

THE RISE OF POPULISM

THERE IS NOTHING WRONG WITH WANTING TO BE POPULAR. THERE'S A LOT WRONG WITH DECEIVING THE ELECTORATE SO AS TO BECOME SO.

The words 'populism' and 'populistic' are thrown about by media outlets that are themselves amongst the most guilty of populism. Some media outlets persistently use, exploit and perhaps create fear, scandal and populistic rhetoric to sell papers. Some use the word 'populist' to discredit any politician who is popular and whose political position differs from their editorial agenda. Any politician able to draw and mobilise a crowd and, God help him or her if also staunch Brexiteer, will almost certainly be labelled populist.

And ask yourself, why is it that a pro-Brexit rally is labelled 'populist', but a People's Vote rally is not?

'Populistic' is a label generally used by three groups. They are not the same but overlap. Those three groups are 1) Social liberals including those in the media, 2) those campaigning to stop the UK's departure from the EU and 3) politicians defending their popularity against the popularity of others. All three use the label 'populistic' in an attempt to marginalise and discredit political opponents who do appeal to the populous.

The problem is that the term is bandied about and misused.

There is nothing in itself wrong with creating appeal, but the term populist as it has been used in recent years implies a political approach based on soundbites rather than serious intent. One could be forgiven for thinking that this applies to 95% of politicians of all hews.

It is truly an irony that the media, politicians and activists who use the term populist in a derogatory sense, do so with the intent of themselves gaining popularity and popular support for their agenda. Those that use the term 'populist' in a critical sense are, by the simple fact that they are employing the term, surely in almost all cases themselves being populistic. Indeed, the use of any emotive language or terminology is perhaps intrinsically populistic. Churchill, by deliberately employing language likely to trigger an emotional reaction to his speeches so as to increase their appeal, could be termed populistic. The ability to rouse the population to great endeavours requires an appeal to people's emotions and passion. Unfortunately, negative emotions are the easiest to exploit and that is why so much political rhetoric and media reporting focuses on bad news, sometimes even appealing to, and even fuelling concerns that, in turn, highlight divisions, raise tensions and thereby, intentional or otherwise, generate fear, frustration and animosity.

It is a rare politician who can rouse an audience with positive words. Even Churchill exploited fear - the menace of NAZI Germany was, in fact, a menace, but it was in highlighting that and exploiting the fear of defeat, that he was able to rouse the nation.

Surely, the truth is that every politician would like to be popular. Being popular creates influence, secures votes from the people, so what politician does not want to be more popular than the other politician? Isn't trying to increase ones' popularity an intrinsic part of politics and democracy? Of course, it is. There is nothing wrong with being popular.

However, there is something very wrong in deceiving the electorate; in creating or inventing reasons for people to feel negative emotions towards others, towards institutions, ideas or scenarios, to then exploit those emotions politically.

It is lacking in integrity to alter what you promise to different audiences simply to be popular to everyone. Such an approach is beyond insincere, it is intrinsically dishonest. Should such a politician ever be in a position of power and expected to implement those policies, they will be caught out, as indeed they frequently are. In that case, the trust of the population in the individual, his/her party and the 'system' will be damaged.

Does that sound familiar? We are already in such a situation. Politicians have been acting in this grossly irresponsible manner for some years. The negative campaigning on both sides of the Brexit campaign deliberately invented baseless risks, over-emphasised the negative impact of staying in and of leaving the European Union, so much so that the term 'Project Fear' was coined.

Frequently, politicians have stood for election on a manifesto that they do not agree with, support or have any intention of implementing. They are no different to someone who lies on their job application form or falsifies the benefits of a particular product to persuade you to buy it. They are men and women of little substance and very little political integrity.

A party manifesto should properly, rightly and confidently considered by the public and all those who seek election based upon it, as the party's work plan proposal to the British people and electorate. However, manifestos have become vehicles of voter persuasion; they are a tool by which to win a vote, not a serious offer or proposal to the people.

The prevalent attitude of national politicians appears to the public to be one of "I'll promise whatever I have to, to become popular – to get the votes I need to win the seat – and I'll worry about delivering what I've promised later".

The result is that, perhaps more so than at any other time, voters no longer believe party manifestos. They have become almost meaningless. However, the electorate has little or nothing else to inform the votes it casts. Is it any surprise that the public is so cynical of politicians, or that people have lost trust in our political system.

Politicians who seek to be popular by making promises that they have no intention of keeping; no intention of implementing, or have not thought through, are simply dishonest.

It is intrinsically dishonest and lacking in integrity to promise something that you have not fully considered, may not be able to deliver or have no intention of implementing. Such politicians should not be called populist. I call them dishonest and unscrupulous.

It is easy to rouse a crowd to passion if you are gifted in rhetoric and a great and passionate orator. It is, however, the height of irresponsibility and disservice to your country and your supporters to rouse a crowd to action when you then intend to leave them to their own devices once they have served your purpose.

There are such politicians active on the fringes today. Steven Yaxley-Lennon aka Tommy Robinson was one. Gerard

Batten, my successor as leader of UKIP, is another. Jeremy Corbyn's entirely unrealistic deployment of 'Father Christmas' policies in the 2019 election was a classic example. His promises to provide so much for nothing would and could never have been implemented had he come to be elected. His aim was to bribe voters in order to win. Most probably his agenda as a prime minister would then have been to build Marxist concepts into the British Constitution.

Claims made by the Brexit party in the summer of 2019, that it would invest £200bn in the regions and would obtain the funds to do so by axing the HS2 rail link (£55-80bn), reducing the foreign aid budget by half (£7bn) and refusing to pay the £39bn 'divorce payment' that Theresa May promised to pay the European Union, simply did not add up. There was a shortfall of up to £97bn in their sums, surely too much to be accidental. That, at the time, was more than the equivalent of the entire defence and education budgets (£29bn and £63.5bn respectively) combined. In my opinion that Brexit Party announcement was knowingly thin, but that wasn't its point. It aim was to broaden the party's popular appeal.

If the calculation was indeed based on knowingly unsound assumptions or figures and was deliberately presented to increase polling figures, the tactic undermines their credibility; if accidental, does the public want people in power who make such risky assumptions about their electoral offer?

The Brexit Party could have done a great deal better than that. If it had done it could have been a serious challenger the Conservative and Labour parties and indeed, could have achieved its aim to "change the way we do politics". Time will tell whether it can rebuild its potential.

The Liberal Democrats chose an entirely populistic

approach in its decision to oppose and, if necessary, overturn and reverse Brexit. The decision was aimed at garnering the support of the 48% who voted to remain in the EU and, in doing so, reinvigorate the Party's finances and fortunes. It thought that it could in some way replicate its popularity in opposing the second Iraq War. This strategic decision was an entirely legitimate one, but it meant that the Party abandoned its traditional liberal and democratic principles. It became the antithesis of the Brexit Party. Neither party faired well.

My primary point is that being populist is not an indication of electoral performance and doesn't necessarily mean the electorate perceive a populist as fit, ready or able to govern the country effectively.

A politician's electoral credentials and those of his or her party must be based upon their offer to the people (their manifesto or work plan) - the 'how', the detail - and their realistic ability and determination to deliver it.

The majority of voters, thankfully, do want a sense of a party's ability to actually deliver. They want to know 'how'. Populism, alone, without credible detail of 'how', is unlikely ever to get a politician into a position of real power.

However, some people do get easily caught up in the cult of populistic causes and figures. They vote for snake oil salesmen and and always will. They will be condemned to wondering why things never change and to being constantly disappointed by 'the establishment' that both they and those they follow will always blame for their failure.

17

THE HARMFUL POLITICS OF IDENTITY & THE MISTAKE OF MULTICULTURISM

BOILED FROGS AND PRIDE IN IDENTIFYING AS BRITISH

We in the UK have a long and successful history of campaigning for people's rights and equal opportunities.

The result is that there is a well established principle in British society that everyone should expect to be treated fairly, equally and that have the same opportunities in education, work and leisure. Society rightly riles at any exception.

In recent years, however, we have seen a rise in so called 'identity politics'. This and multiculturalism, which is closely related, are factionalising society and compromising the principle of equity for all.

Identity means not only what you are, but also what others are not. Identity exists only where there are socially recognised differences. To emphasise identity is to emphasis the differences between those who share the same identity and those who do not.

Frequently, identity politics are related to social inequality or perceived bad treatment in whatever way. This can lead, in a political sense, to a defensive, protective and sometimes adversarial posture being adopted by identity campaigners.

Group identity requires members of the group to establish exclusion. Not only exclusion from their group of others who are different, but also to exclude themselves from other groups

In Kosovo in the 1990's the Albanians withdrew themselves from state education. In doing so they excluded themselves from a collective system and created a new difference that reinforced their identity separate to that of the Serbs. They portrayed their non-participation in the state system as having been excluded from it, when in reality they excluded themselves. In that way they also created an identity of being oppressed; they added to the identity of the Serbian State as the oppressor. They enhanced their identity on a number of levels: education, exclusion from the state, victimisation/oppression (at best exaggerated, at worst manufactured) and the West fell for it. It was a master-lesson in weaponising identity politics.

We see similar methods, albeit a great deal less dramatic and hostile, in identity campaigns in the UK and the US. Differences of ethnicity, gender, race, religion, place of origin, language, politics and indeed on Brexit are highlighted not only in the form of what members of the group have in common. They also exclude other identities from their group and reject the concept of their own integration into broader society because, to accept integration breaks down differences and dilutes the political power of identity. They emphasise differences and grievances, sometimes over emphasising them to make a point and to trigger an emotional response that helps them to accrue financial, popular and political support. The attention they get can overshadow other groups who, as a result, feel sidelined and under represented in the debate.

Even victims have become an identity. People who are not victims are, it is claimed in some quarters, unable to understand or comprehend the plight of victims. As such the opinions of 'non-victims' are, it is argued, irrelevant. Being a victim, it seems, now, through this approach, conveys political influence.

The Me Too movement, a network of victims and survivors of alleged sexual harassment and assault, is an example. At the time of writing, the headline of the Me To Movement website is "You are not alone". It is indisputable that such a headline is comforting but also identity related. It is inclusive of victims and excludes those who are not victims. The headline may as well be 'you are one, they are not'.

The Men Too movement emphasises not only the plight of victims (a good thing), but also their difference to everyone else. In reality such divisions are rarely so well defined. Life and sexual interaction is not so simple.

Furthermore, the 'us and them' attitude and politicisation of 'victim-hood' has resulted in a surge not only in real victims feeling more confident about speaking up (again a very good thing), but also in a which-hunt against men whose behaviour is alleged but unproven to have been unacceptable. And what is acceptable? What is unacceptable and in what contexts? Who defines it? Who decides? Context, including the behaviour and motivation of the 'victim' is often disregarded.

The politicisation of victims thorough the introduction of

identity politics does a massive disservice to the victims themselves. For example the politicisation of the issue was directly responsible for Home Office policy that investigators should assume the honesty of supposed victims. This in turn led to some high profile cases which resulted in men losing their reputation and careers only to have been later, too late, proven to be innocent. Such examples include those of Field Marshall Lord Edwin Bramall and Leon Britton. How does such a political policy in any way assist the cause of supporting victims? It actually creates victims.

There is an argument that false accusations are less common than truthful ones. This may be true, but it is a grossly unfair and unjust position to hold. A maliciously false allegation can destroy lives, as it did in the cases of Bramall and Brittan.

There is also powerful argument that the Me Too Movement creates an inaccurate and unhelpful impression that women are vulnerable and helpless prey. Women are as capable of being sexual predators as men are and some do play on their sexuality in attempts to gain access or advantage.

The name of the 'Black Lives Matter' campaign against violence and systemic racism towards black people could be taken to imply that white lives do not matter. The name creates an identity around race and the right to life.

Of course, I realise and fully appreciate that the origin and name of the movement is in response to a perception that black lives matter less than others. Indeed, historically that was often the case. Moreover, such prejudice, appallingly, still does exist in some parts of the world.

However, the name 'Black Lives Matter' certainly serves to

emphasise and so enhance racial differences and in doing so reinforces black identity and enables political exploitation. So, the question has to be asked, is the name political. Does this serve the alleged purpose of the movement well?

The fact is that all lives matter.

As all lives matter, wouldn't the title 'Everyone's Life Matters' be a significantly more positive, constructive, unifying and likely to yield positive change? Would that not encourage the erosion of the differences that brought about the need for the movement in the first place? Whereas the title 'Black Lives Matter' actually highlights and reinforces them?

I support any aim to reduce real exploitation, victimisation, violence, prejudice and division. But identity campaigns have a responsibility to address their concerns in such a manner as to reduce differences and strengthen social understanding, unity and cohesion, rather than highlight, emphasise and build differences. And let's be real about it, if a campaign can trigger animosity and a sense of being ignored, oppressed or victimised it is damaging society, but it can also gain significant support. Highlighting differences and injustices is an effective campaigning technique. Society must be cautious of movements of that sort, however meritorious their aim, that deepen rather than erode social divisions.

The tendency towards establishing multiple group identities within broader society appears to be growing. Not only growing, but the differences that identity politics highlight, the exclusions that result and the barriers they create, are increasingly accepted as they become more common and as 'political correctness' deters the expression of any concerns. This situation reminds one of the boiled frog analogy.

Please do not try this, but, is one places a frog in boiling water it will, of course, leap out. However, place a frog in cold water and heat it slowly and the frog will adapt to the changing temperature and stay where it is, until, apparently it dies.

The boiling frog analogy is a lesson that adaptation is not necessarily a good thing; that thinking that we are adapting and that therefore all is and will be well is dangerous.

The fact that we have become used to the fictionalisation of society, to its declining coherence and unity, is not an indictor that all is well.

Public bodies and authorities have been reinforcing the disintegration of society, undermining the unity and cohesion of the broader community.

At the end of January 2019, it was revealed that a particular regional fire service introduced a recruitment policy requiring 60% of recruits to be women, and 35% to be from black and minority ethnic groups by 2021. Reportedly, white men had to score seven out of ten in the numerical, verbal and mechanical reasoning exam to get through to the next stage – a physical test – while women and BME candidates only had to score six out of ten.

Does it matter whether the man, woman, lesbian, homosexual or trans-sexual rescuing someone from a fire is from a black, minority or ethnic group; what country they were born in; what their religion is, or whether they are atheist? They could come from the moon for all most of us needing their help would care.

We should expect only one thing from our fire and other emergency services in this regard: that they recruit the very best people for the job, regardless of the sex, ethnicity, colour or religion of the candidate.

However, to be fair, the fire service in question was responding to the broader growth in 'Identity Politics' that has infected our entire society and administration. For example, the Fire and Rescue Service Equality and Diversity Strategy: 2008–2018, contains a great deal of good, solid direction regarding equal opportunities. That said, it also states:

"By 2013, a minimum of 15 per cent of new entrants to the operational sector to be women."

"By 2013, recruitment of minority ethnic staff across the whole organisation to be at the same percentage as the minority ethnic representation in the local working population."

The reality is that equal - proportional may be a better word - representation policies of this sort ignore the fact that we are not all the same; that we have different strengths as well as weaknesses, that different communities hold different social perspectives and, importantly, that we make different choices.

It is true that the choices some people make may be influenced by inequalities in society, and the fears and prejudices experienced by some groups must be addressed. But the concept of 'multiculturalism' highlights and sustains the identity differences between communities, social perspectives and choices.

In doing so, multiculturalism is, in large part responsible for the rise in identity politics, which then leads to the demand for equal representation. This, in turn, undermines equal opportunities which, in turn, then feeds identity awareness and politics. It is a vicious circle that has to be broken.

The Fire and Rescue service is far from alone, however, it is illustrative.

Because they were required to meet a higher standard due to their identity, white men wanting to join the fire

Service seemingly faced gender and ethnic discrimination and fewer opportunities than candidates with different genetic characteristics. Is that fair? Should not all firefighters, police officers, soldiers, sailors, airmen and everyone applying for any job, meet the same standards of selection?

I care greatly that our emergency services select the very best candidates rather than prioritise those possessing any specific BME, gender or sexual characteristics. The fact is that incorporating these terms into recruitment policies is in itself divisive. The reality is that identity politics and any policy of prioritising identity and equal representation over competence places us all at increased risk of harm when applied to the emergency services.

And what about the person who gets lower marks than someone else, but still gets the job because they are identified with a different gender or BME group? How should they feel about that? Are they likely to feel proud and experience a sense of achievement, or will they potentially feel insecure when working with junior colleagues who may have achieved higher standards but didn't get the promotion?

What about the person who gets the higher marks, but is rejected because they are not from one of the preferred 'identity groups'? How should we expect them to feel? Does that encourage satisfaction or does it potentially lead to sense bitterness and prejudice?

What is positive in this? Does it contribute anything towards breaking down divisions?

Of course, it does not. It achieves the opposite. It highlights differences and creates divisions. Indeed, it's no different to when I first applied for an army commission. I scored very highly in all my tests, only to be told that I came from the wrong background and school and therefore wouldn't be going forward. I'm sure you'd agree that was unfair and wrong. It was an example of identity politics and no different to West Midlands Fire Service recruitment objectives as reported in January 2019.

I finally passed out from Sandhurst as a Territorial Army officer, ten years later, as Best Overall Cadet.

The socially divisive influence of identity politics is, of course, fed by those who wish to highlight their own identity. The LGBTQ community, for example, makes a point of establishing and highlighting its exclusive identity as a community.

With Gay Pride, the LGBTQ community is sending the message - deliberately or not, is of little importance - "you share our identity and are one of us, or you are not". From whatever angle you look at that, it is divisive and gives rise to calls for tongue in cheek, but similarly divisive calls for 'heterosexual' or 'straight pride'.

Those of us excluded from Gay Pride are subjected to the 'rainbow flag being flown from government buildings, having our streets closed, and our trains, police cars and pedestrian crossings repainted in the rainbow colours.

It is this kind of phenomenon, applied also to race, that triggered the appearance in December 2019 of posters in Perth stating "It's ok to be white". Police Scotland were investigating the case as a possible instance of hate crime. Would they be dong so if the posters said "It's ok to be black"? Is it not ok to be white?

It is easy to see, in examples such as this, how the generally well meaning attempts to remove prejudice can actually, if not well thought through and if based on identity, exacerbate divisions.

The British Isles is a melting pot of identities. It has

always been an evolving, constantly morphing mix of immigrants and cultures: Celts, Romans, Anglo-Saxons, Jutes, Vikings, Normans, Huguenots, Indians, Pakistanis, West Indians, Poles... Indeed, regional variations within the United Kingdom were massive and remain a characteristic of our nation. For example, the variations between the characteristics of the Highland and Lowland Scots. However, until quite recently, there has always been a melding of these, a coming together, a peaceful coexistence and a process of assimilation and adaptation. Differences have not so much had dividing lines, but vaguely defined and melded regional variations. This has led to friendly rivalry and banter. It has added to the character of our people and, perhaps, our resilience. We have all benefited in terms of language, cuisine, art and a broader understanding of the wider world, whether that world is the other side of the Pennines, in the next county or the Indian sub-continent. It gives us character, knowledge, ideas and healthy rivalry. This is all to the good.

The term 'multiculturalism' originally meant maintaining socially, ethnically and diverse cultures within one community.

However, the term has, in popular language if not in the dictionaries, been hardened. It now implies the right of each self-identifying group in a to defend and preserve its identity as something different to all the others. As such groups have been allowed, encouraged even, to define their identities in relation to others, the blurred and soft boundaries between groups that mitigate abrasiveness and confrontation and allow acceptance and albeit sometimes passionate but friendly rivalry, are being replaced with stark, divisions.

Soft, melded boundaries where the point of overlap

between communities, whether geographical, social or cultural or all three, reduces tension between them.

However, sharp, well defined and contrasting divisions can create bitter rivalry and competition, abrasiveness, tension, prejudice and conflict.

The term multiculturalism has also been used by what I shall call the 'equal representationalists'. Both here and in the United States multiculturalism has been twisted by those who seek to sharpen the definitions of different groups and communities within one legal and administrative jurisdiction e.g. the UK. No longer are immigrants expected to enter the melting pot of British society and to participate in the evolutionary process of assimilation.

Indeed, reflecting this, in August 2019, Neil Basau, at the time the Metropolitan Police Assistant Commissioner, was reported as saying that Muslims in the UK should not have to assimilate [into broader UK society?].

As 'to assimilate' means "to become part of a group, country or society", Mr Basau seems to have been reinforcing a growing school of opinion that Muslims and, indeed, other 'identities' shouldn't have to become members of our broader 'melting pot' society.

To accept 'non-assimilation multiculturalism' is to accept a patchwork of communities, divided by their attempts to defy assimilation and to do so by highlighting their different characteristics: gender, sexuality, religion, colour, society or origin, language etc.

Once these divisions, particularly in cases of religion and ethnicity, gain geographical associations the process inevitably influences local politics. Frequently, Muslims will vote for a Muslim candidate, BME communities for BME candidates and so on. This reinforces and further politicises identity differences and in doing so further challenges assimilation of all people into one homogenous society.

Of course, everyone should have political representation. The question I pose is, should every separate cultural, racial, ethnic, religious, gender, sexual or linguistic community be represented as such - which seems to be a tendency at present - or should all politicians be safeguarding the interests of all our people regardless of identity? Should they care about identity, or should the care about everyone regardless of identity?

For the sake of debate, if, as a nation, we accept patchwork multiculturalism and culturally based political representation as being the way forward, can we look to anywhere else in the world to find such politics and to see what this might involve?

The answer is yes, we can. One country that has de facto identity based politics and political representation is Kenya.

In Kenya, when votes are cast, tribal and ethnic affiliation plays a crucial part. The stakes for individual communities are therefore huge as they compete for political advantage. In 2007, public disorder and clashes between the larger ethnic tribes, the Kikuyus, Luos and Kalenjins, erupted after a Kikuyu community leader was declared the winner in elections amidst accusations of rigging and electoral manipulation. In such cases, the losing communities are politically sidelined and frequently suppressed by the winning one that wields the greatest authority.

Similar examples to that of Kenya can be found in Central Asia, the Russian Federation, the United States and indeed most of the world. I am not suggesting that the UK is on the verge of inter-ethnic violence, however, the politicisation of identity along cultural lines is a trend that is gaining traction here in the UK too. Let us not emulate these practices simply because they exist elsewhere.

It is not, of course, ethnicity, or any other community identity or affiliation itself that is the problem. The problem arises when community leaders, politicians, activists or agitators, at any level, use identity for their personal gain or naively and, in doing so create divisions which breed yet further division and identity based exclusions.

I may be accused of ranting, but it cannot be repeated enough that identity politics are inherently harmful in the context of broader society. Identity politics create discrimination and encourage and deepen prejudices and divisions rather than reduce them.

The politics of identity, through demanding equal representation, undermine standards and excellence in all areas of life: healthcare, business and commerce, education, the armed and emergency services, and government.

To avoid any misunderstanding, I re-state that whilst identity politics are inherently harmful, merit based equal opportunities are a good thing and must always be pursued and if necessary fought for.

To be a truly successful and vibrant nation we must build and support a united, cohesive, caring and meritocratic society that able to evolve and adapt and build its character as a nation.

To remove discrimination we must oppose identity politics wherever and whenever we come across them. We must instead demand merit based equal opportunities and argue that the best suited, most enthusiastic person gets the job, not the one who helps meet some politically correct, identity based but damaging, statistics based, tick-box target that enables politicians to give smooth answers.

Let us not accept the continued habit of immigrant communities bringing their identity politics to the UK. It is almost inevitable that immigrant communities will instinctively seek to do so, but not because they wish to do so. In many cases they will have left their country of origin as a direct result of the impact of, and instability and insecurity caused by identity based politics there.

It is also crucial that all politicians recognise reality. That is, everyone has strengths, and everyone has weaknesses. We must reject identity politics and equal representation as an objective, no matter what attempts may be made to justify it. Instead, we must encourage assimilation without oppression. We must pursue equal opportunities.

We must do far more to support everyone, regardless of age or any racial, gender, sexual, cultural or other characteristics, to identify, build upon and exploit their individual strengths and opportunities for the benefit of both themselves and society as a whole. We must end the suppression of excellence and recognise that, with the right support, everyone can be excellent, but in different areas and not in all things.

Our education system has a crucial role to play, however, it, like our politicians, has fundamentally failed in this respect and must be reformed accordingly.

Rather than encouraging and helping people to develop their individual strengths and abilities and helping them to identify, increase and exploit their opportunities, our schools perpetuate the myth that we are all the same, dumbing down excellence. We know we are not all the same.

Herein lies the apparent contradiction: to build a fairer society that rejects identity politics and discrimination, and in order to provide everyone with equal opportunities, we have to recognise that we are not equal in all things; that we are all different.

It is not actually a contradiction.

The answer lies in recognising that what we, as individuals, have to offer society is not based on our group identity – our gender, sexual orientation, ethnicity, race or anything else – it is based upon our own character, skills, ability and work ethic as individual human beings.

As a society, we should look at the person: their individual strengths, their development and the contribution they can make. We must not do as the proponents of identity politics and equal representation would have us do; we must not highlight and perpetuate the differences and divisions in society and undermine the value of merit by focusing on the group that a person can or wishes to be identified with.

If we are to create a socially coherent, confident and optimistic society in the UK, we must reject the increasing definition of differences and delineations between us and instead build on the strengths of that we all bring to the team. This means rejecting patchwork multiculturalism, identity politics and equal representation. Instead, we must embrace variety, continue to fight for equal opportunities and condemn those who bring socially divisive traits to politics too create and exploit divisions within our nation.

Finally on this subject, in which I have explored what identity politics are and why they are harmful, I pose a couple of questions. Before I do, it is worth reminding ourselves that we all need to feel a sense of belonging; the sense of being a part of something bigger than ourselves. It is that sense that drives our search for an identity. So, my question is:

"Does the decline in national pride - in being British -

driven in large part by those who have condemned our history (Chapter 3), mean that there is no longer an overarching identity that unites all the people of these islands, however otherwise diverse they may be? Is it this that has driven people to seek and assert identities unrelated to our community as a whole?"

18

THE DANGER OF DOCTRINE

AND THE NEED FOR SOMETHING NEW

Many politicians dogmatically adhere to and apply the principles of a particular doctrine, rather than concern themselves with the delivery of positive change. They may believe their political doctrine or ideology to be the best, but their decisions and actions are often directed by adherence to them, rather than an appreciation of the effect on real world situations.

Let me explain.

Many Conservatives are adherents to the principles of 'Economic Conservatism'. That means they believe that to govern responsibly the government must lower taxes, reduce government spending, minimise involvement in the economy and privatise or outsource public services. They believe that is what good conservatives do.

Many Labour MPs are 'Economic Socialists'. They believe that the government must be prominent in economic and commercial life, managing the economy to reduce the wealth gap and to protect worker's rights. Some see this as the first step in achieving a Marxist type, classless society.

Libertarian politicians - and there are such in a number of parties - are a broad bunch. Essentially, they advocate maximising individual rights and minimising the role of the state. Some believe in an uncompromising level of individualism and place little or no emphasis on social interaction or cooperation. Other libertarians are more extreme and tend toward anarchy. They are highly sceptical of authority, believe that the state interferes with individual liberties and should, in an ideal world, be abolished in terms of its influence in people's lives.

It is important to recognise that privatisation is a defining characteristic of economic conservatism. A strict adherent to economic conservatism is convinced that market forces produce the most efficient results. Therefore, if he or she sees a service being delivered by the state they will seek to privatise or outsource it, simply because that is what they believe should happen. They don't necessarily relate it to a defined end state measured by positive effect for ordinary people, commerce, the local and national economies, or security.

Of course, such a dogmatic and unimaginative approaches to politics avoids the inconvenience of having to acknowledge that different people, communities and businesses face specific challenges and therefore need bespoke solutions. Blind pursuit of doctrine requires little analysis or thinking, it is the easy or lazy approach and it encourages an 'ivory tower' attitude that isolates politicians from the real every day world of ordinary people. For some MPs, that can be a very comfortable position.

Any politician who pursues the goal of implementing a political ideology, philosophy or doctrine, whatever it is, without understanding and judging the 1st, 2nd and 3rd order effects of every decision on the confidence, optimism, prosperity and security of ordinary people, communities and businesses, is a politician whose eye is not focused on the delivery of positive change. In practical terms, they mistake the means as an end in itself and, in my view, are not fit for office.

In the 18th century, the industrial revolution caused tectonic changes in society and political thinking responded. Modern socialism, conservatism and liberalism all grew out of the specific economic and social conditions that emerged over the following 150 years or so. They represented different social classes and, in their various ways, attempted to address the issues of the time, including worker's rights and the growing social and economic divisions in society.

Unquestionably the last forty years have seen new and significant influences on society, one of global dimensions and at least as significant as the industrial revolution, the second and third influences are more specific to the United Kingdom, although not uniquely so.

The first is the technology and the worldwide web. Technology and new discoveries have changed the raw materials we use, how they are exploited, the way food is produced and the way in which goods are manufactured. The traditional, industrial working class has all but disapeared from British society.

The internet has revolutionised social interaction and the quantity of information that is now available to everyone. The speed at which communication takes place and the extent to which information can be manipulated, honestly and dishonestly, to communicate, but also to manipulate perceptions, opinions, ideas and beliefs, influences thousands or even millions of people.

The second influence has been a growing emphasis, in

the West, on economic and social liberalism. This has caused a significant trend towards material self-interest at a cost to the cohesiveness of society as a whole. Social liberal attitudes have, in some quarters, given rise to the idea that altruism is actually unwise.

The third influence has been the impact of libertarianism. This has strengthened individual freedoms (a good thing), but undermined social responsibility, interaction and cooperation, respect for authority, the rule of law and a sense of community (a bad thing).

Whether judged as positive or negative these influences have triggered massive changes over the last few decades. Not least, the traditional working class base of the Labour Party has declined dramatically, leaving the Labour Party confused as to its core audience and purpose. Yet, despite these tectonic changes, the only political tools we have at our disposal to cope with them are those political parties, ideologies, philosophies and doctrines that grew out of the 18th and 19th centuries. They emerged at a time when a very different society required other political solutions to those we need now. This is not to say that socialism, liberalism and conservatism no longer have a place, but that they are not now so generally appropriate and that we do now need something new.

Government, our parliament and devolved administrations must better address the needs of a new era. It is an era of a more culturally and less financially diverse, but increasingly disunited population, with a far weaker sense of national identity or the greater good and with hugely powerful social communications available.

A new political philosophy is required for the circumstances of 21st century Britain.

That philosophy must be based on the principle that it is the task of the law, government and public administration to enhance the confidence, optimism, prosperity and security of all individuals, communities, businesses; of the entire nation.

Whether a nation and its people are confident, optimistic, prosperous and secure can be measured and assessed in a number of ways, however, they are also feelings. If an individual, community or population feels confident, optimistic, prosperous and secure, they are most likely going to be content with the state of their society and the efficacy of their government.

These terms are in the main self explanatory, however, it is important to realise that they all interrelate. If a person feels prosperous and secure for example, they are well on the way to also feeling confident and optimistic. For this reason, no policy should be developed in isolation of others. There is a complex matrix of cause and effect: do one thing over here and it will inevitably have second or third order implications over there. These may be positive, negative or neutral in impact, but they must be understood and managed. This is why strategic grasp and acumen are such crucial attributes in any leading politician.

The term 'security' perhaps is the one that requires expansion.

When I talk of security, I do not simply mean security in a military or policing sense, or that of the preservation of life and property, although I do include those things.

I also mean the sense of emotional security; the actual feeling of being secure in society, work, education and healthcare; the knowledge of living in a stable social, cultural and natural environment, free of imposed and overly rapid change, complex stresses, worries and anxieties. A secure environment is also one that allows freedom of speech, opinion and expression without suppression of any sort; one that provides equal access to justice and is governed by the needs of the individual, communities and businesses rather than by the imposition of ever more complex, impersonal processes and the transfer of the financial burden from the centre to those already struggling.

You will now see that confidence, optimism, prosperity and security are separate, but intimately related. I shall repeat that policies at all levels of government must recognise that fact and be designed accordingly.

The appropriateness of decisions may be measured by the extent to which they contribute, directly or indirectly, towards material and emotional confidence, optimism, prosperity and security.

Achieving this level of delivery requires strategic vision, acumen and leadership and so, a new breed of politician.

Career orientated, dogmatic or unscrupulous politicians, or those who need processes, procedures and directions to function, simply cannot cut it. Party mouthpieces, unable to identify and define problems and design bespoke solutions on behalf of the constituents and nation they represent, are unfit to grace the green or the red benches in Westminster.

If we can reach a point at which politicians and political parties are truly able to free themselves from dogma and orientate themselves towards delivering positive effect in the lives of individuals, communities and businesses, they may then be properly judged by the electorate on their ability to do so.

I call this political approach 'Social Prosperetism'.

19

LIBERAL EXTREMISM AND THE PROBLEM OF THE LEFT/RIGHT SPECTRUM

WHY THE CONCEPT OF THE LEFT / RIGHT SPECTRUM IS INAPPROPRIATE , MISLEADING AND DAMAGING TO OUR POLITICS

The 'left-right' spectrum that politicians, political commentators in the media or elsewhere and ordinary people refer to, is a problem. It skews our perspective of politics. It creates a frame for our thinking that constrains political imagination and is therefore unhelpful in addressing political issues in the modern era.

The labelling of political parties, politicians and activists as *left*, *right* or *centre*, is misleading and a fundamental obstacle in uniting a post Brexit UK or in building political consensus on almost any issue. The left-right concept is a polarising one. Left and right are opposites.

The terms left and right, in politics, have their origins in the French revolutionary parliamentary assembly in which the aristocracy sat to the right of the speaker of the assembly and the commoners on his left. Sitting on the right implied support for the pre-revolutionary 'old order' things, the aristocracy and royalty; sitting on the left implied support for republicanism, secularism and civil liberties.

In a physical sense, that layout did not accommodate any

political position between its two wings, either in general or on specific issues.

So, to accommodate more subtle political positions, left and right have become a linear spectrum with infinite points between the extremities. Those midway between the two are said to be in the centre.

It is easy to see, given this framing of political positions, how those occupying the 'centre' of politics could easily come to regard individuals, policies or parties furthest from them, either to the left or the right, as extreme and, the further to the left or right, the more extreme they appear.

It is interesting to observe that the terms left, centre and right, allow for the term *extremist* to be applied to those on the extremities on the left and right, but not to those in the centre who are virtually immune from the label.

People who claim association with the centre of the political spectrum are able to argue that they are not at the extremities and therefore are not extreme. They argue that they are, by implication, rational people who hold rational views. This in turn generates the entirely unreliable assumption that they are moderates, that they can see all sides of an argument and offer a political 'middle-way'. This is, of course, absolute rubbish. But psychologically it works. It is difficult, if we accept the concept of the left-right spectrum, to label people, politics or parties in the centre as extremist or irrational. Yet, clearly, those in the centre can be just as extreme, moderate, rational or irrational as those anywhere else on the political spectrum.

Indeed, it is worth recalling the inherent contradictions within the UK's traditional centre party, the Liberal Democrats. The LibDems call themselves "radical". Yet the word moderate is the antonym, or opposite, of radical. The terms radical and moderate are inherently contradictory and their application in the description of one party is entirely nonsensical.

However, from the centre, it is very easy to criticise ideas, policies, individuals or political parties that are distanced from the centre.

If we one accepts, consciously or not, the idea that the centre is occupied by rational, moderate and compromising people who can see everything around them, then the further anyone else is from the middle the more irrational, blinkered and bigoted they are assumed to be, and the easier it is to label them as such. When that happens, the value and relevance of their opinions, ideas and concerns, which are in reality very rarely unreasonable or unfounded, are immediately undermined and a large swathe of the population disenfranchised in terms of national debate.

The reality, of course, is that there is extremism in all things. There are extreme views concerning liberty, freedom of speech, human rights and liberalism. There are extreme means that can, and are sometimes applied in pursuance of otherwise 'liberal' or centre ground principles, values and ideals.

There are also significant contradictions and hypocrisies in the way that we think of politics. A person may argue passionately for the freedom to practice religion but simultaneously refuse to criticise religions that are themselves, highly discriminatory and restrictive of human rights and freedoms.

We think of liberalism as sitting in the middle of the political spectrum. So, what is liberalism?

There is 'classical liberalism', 'social liberalism', 'economic liberalism', 'new liberalism', 'neoliberalism' and 'political liberalism'. Then there is the imported American concept of liberalism.

The Liberal Democrats espouse social liberalism. However, confusingly, there are people across the political spectrum and in all major political parties in the UK, who describe themselves as social liberals. Perhaps it is these people who are the cause of many political difficulties today. They pursue whatever politics they wish, extreme or otherwise, whilst simultaneously claiming to be 'socially liberal', thereby donning the cloak of moderate, open-minded and rational rationalism they believe the term implies.

Such people may argue passionately for freedom of expression and speech, but exercise great intolerance towards any political view that does not match their own. They claim to abhor oppression and state interference in their lives, but themselves employ intimidation, derogatory labels, language and insults to suppress political views and ideas that contradict or challenge their own.

Classical liberalism is at variance with social liberalism. It advocates the right of every person to live their life free from interference from anyone else, with the crucial caveat that, in doing so, they do not interfere with the ability of others to live free lives. The ticklish, and uncomfortable implication of this is that, at some point, there must be a willingness to support intervention, forceful if necessary, to enforce the caveat. Furthermore, those who are called upon and whose duty it is to intervene to uphold classical liberal values in extreme circumstances of confrontation and conflict e.g. police officers, armed forces personnel and aid workers, sacrifice their own protection as offered under the classical liberal principle. They are voluntarily giving up their ability to live their life according to their wishes in order to uphold and protect the right of others to do so. This is an uncomfortable concept for some social liberals, but not classical liberals. Classical liberals accept the concept of sacrifice for the greater good. Social liberals are less keen on it. The implication that the right of everyone to live their life free from interference requires a preparedness to intervene, often forcefully, to safeguard the concept doesn't necessary sit will with them. This creates a contradiction that social liberals find difficult. Perhaps this is why classical liberalism has, in my view unfortunately, faded in modern political fashion.

Neo-liberalism and economic liberalism in the modern era were ushered in by Margret Thatcher. She believed in a free-market approach to public services based on the sale of publicly owned industries and utilities. This has remained the trade-mark of the Conservative Party policy to this day. Furthermore, as I describe elsewhere, it has become a dogma - this is what modern conservatives do.

There is a tendency to mindlessly out-source public services and utilities; letting the market dictate their character, size and operation. Little thought is given to why. It is simply the done thing if you are a conservative and if you question it you will not be welcome and will most likely get nowhere in the Conservative party.

Libertarianism covers a host of things. I have found people who claim to be passionate 'libertarians', to be confused as to what libertarianism actually is. Whilst there are 'moderate' and 'extreme' libertarians, they all tend to argue passionately for the freedom to do what they want; they are opposed to rules and laws that impinge upon what they define as their personal freedoms, without considering the impact of their own behaviour on broader society. They want and argue for free markets. They see no contradiction between their demand for personal freedom and their wish to see the introduction of tough criminal law, the death penalty and draconian immigration policies, such as the deportation of EU citizens still residing in the UK when we leave the EU. They want til see these things applied to others, but don't want to submit themselves to authority. They advocate the removal human rights legislation from the statute books and a reduction of protections for those they dislike for any reason. They are all united by describing themselves as "anti-establishment". Many verge on anarchistic.

So, can liberalism, in any of its guises, be described as being necessarily moderate. I would say absolutely not.

Liberals may be as extreme, or more so than anyone considered to be on the extremities of either the left or the right.

As in liberalism, as in everything else. There are moderate positions and there are positions of extremes.

Extremists may be found in the supposed centre ground of politics as well as on what we have come to term the left and right. Indeed, those in the centre could be said to provoke animosity between the left and the right forcing them into more extreme responses.

If we fail to recognise this simple fact we will continue to fail in our understanding of why the British people are so divided on almost every topic and why the Brexit debate has been so damaging.

We need an answer to the inherent limitations of the left-right spectrum and the deeply harmful political shaping influence it has had. Failure to identify a new frame for British politics will mean that the goal of a united, confident, optimistic, prosperous and secure nation will elude us.

We must stop seeing politics as a linear spectrum and see

it instead as a centre point from which all views, ideas, ideologies, philosophies, religions and practices radiate in different directions, towards separate destinations.

The linear political spectrum frames politics incorrectly. It places the extremes only on the left and the right. However, the truth, as I have pointed out, is that extremes exist in all thinking and methodology. All politics seek to lead us in different directions towards different destinations and there are many more directions than left, right or straight on.

Here it is maybe useful to remind ourselves as to what 'extreme' actually means. It means:

- Positioned at the furthest point from the centre.
- Excessive.
- Exaggerated, going to exaggerated lengths or using exaggerated methods.
- Exceeding the normal, expected or acceptable.

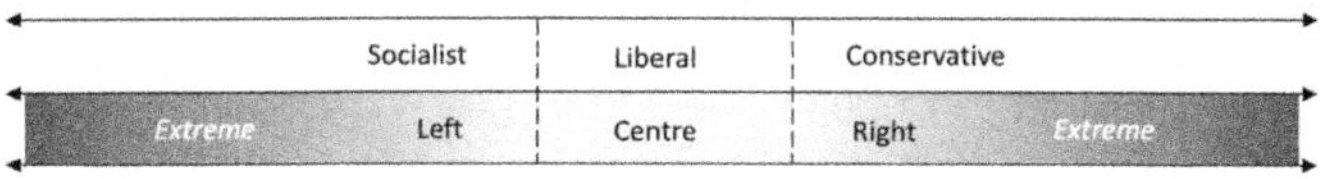

Fig 1: The conventional left/right/centre linear political spectrum

Fig 1: shows the conventional left-right, linear spectrum. It leaves no room for extremism in the centre and it does not allow for extremism in other politically relevant areas or detail such as religion. More than being descriptively inadequate, the linear spectrum frames our political thinking and commentary in such a way that it excludes accurate analysis and realistic, real world decision making.

I advocate a different way of seeing politics and the relative positions of moderate and extreme political views, policies and activism.

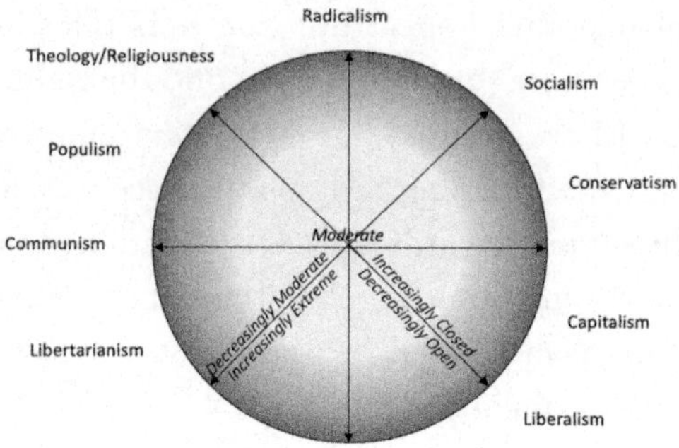

Fig 2: The Political Compass

Fig 2. Shows my proposed 'Political Compass'. Any political 'ism', ideology, philosophy, policy or method may be placed within it.

The compass demonstrates that, from a central point of zero, where no idea, opinion, belief or method exists, all politics may be taken outwards in different directions, diverging towards ever more exaggerated points in relation to the others. As an idea, belief or method develops it moves through a moderate zone towards the extremity. In doing so it can be considered to be increasingly extreme.

On the political compass, no political approach is immune to being extreme. No matter the politics concerned, the closer to the centre of the compass a policy, opinion, method or activity lies, the more moderate it can be considered to be and the closer and more open to the others and their opinions they are.

Conversely, the further from the centre of the circle, something is positioned, the more distant the politics in question are from the others and therefore more extreme and closed to the views of they are.

The Political Compass places politics in a far more realistic context than the misleading left-right spectrum.

The Political Compass provides a far more appropriate and useful analytical frame for understanding and responding to what is going on in 21st century society.

20

NATIONALISM & PATRIOTISM

This very brief chapter seeks simply to offer a definition for two widely misunderstood and misused, perhaps abused, terms.

Nationalism

The habit of identifying oneself with a single nation or other entity, placing it beyond good and evil and recognising no other duty than advancing its interests. Nationalism is inseparable from the desire for power and prestige for the nation or entity in which a person has chosen to create their identity.

Patriotism

Devotion to a particular place and way of life, which one believes to be the best in the world for them but has no wish to force on other people. Patriotism is appreciative of other ways of life but, of its character, is protective of its own, both militarily and culturally.

I am a patriot.

AFTERWORD

The Brexit debate and general election have left the Conservative party, which shed much of its Europhile wing, much changed, Its position on Brexit has consolidated and its majority in Parliament secures its ability to govern without political hindrance.

The Labour Party, left confused and divided as to its purpose following its catastrophic defeat in the 2019 election, has now to reinvent itself. Its position on Brexit was unpopular, as was its leader, Jeremy Corbyn, whose Marxist tendencies raised concerns among traditional Labour voters and whose 'wish list' election manifesto lacked credibility. More importantly perhaps, in the longer term, Labour's working class support base has collapsed. The industrial working class has shrunk with the closure of heavy industry and the run down of manufacturing over recent decades. What industrial working class voters there still are were put off by Corbyn's open lack of patriotism.

Going forward, the signs for Labour are not good and are unlikely to improve until its leaders accept and agree the causes of its defeat in 2019, how to address them, and set a new course for the Party.

UKIP must take the credit for building up the Brexit debate, for bringing about the referendum in 2016 and for the result. However, UKIP committed collective political suicide in 2018 when its NEC manipulated the vote to reject reform, remove me from the leadership and adopt a hard-right stance. Its support collapsed. The Brexit Party picked up the Brexit banner that UKIP had left lying on the ground.

The Brexit Party's subsequent victory in the European election in May 2019 was a pivotal moment. It triggered the resignation of Theresa May and the subsequent election of Boris Johnson as leader of the Conservative and Unionist Party of Great Britain and Northern Ireland. Johnson became Prime Minister and, subsequently, won the 2019 General Election.

The Brexit Party can take much of the credit, therefore, for securing the implementation of the 2016 referendum result - the UK's departure from the EU.

However, The Brexit Party then made a series of disastrous mistakes. The first was the assumption that Boris Johnson would have no choice but to come to some sort of electoral arrangement, pact or deal with them, in the run up to the general election. This assumption was based on gross over-confidence born of the Party's EU election result, very poor and badly blinkered political analysis, and a failure to consider and plan for alternative scenarios, despite being advised to do so.

That assumption, and expectation, of a deal with the Conservatives led to the unwise decision to stand Brexit Party candidates in all constituencies in the general election. The Party even refused to accept, despite it staring them in the face, the evidence of the Pererborough and Brecon & Radnorshire by-election results, which demonstrated clearly that standing candidates in all constituencies would split the pro-Brexit vote, threaten a Conservative majority in the House of Commons and place Brexit at risk.

In the end, as they were always going to, the Conservative Party called Nigel Farage's bluff. They rejected outright any sort of electoral pact. Farage was left with no alternative but to stand down his party's candidates in 317 seats. Done properly: more tactically, with greater attention to detail, with proper political planning and better spin, that move could have secured the position of the Brexit Party and slowed, if not arrested, the Party's slide in the polls. Instead, the 317 seats were crudely selected, allowed closet 'Remainer' Conservative candidates to stand unchallenged and demoralised swathes of Brexit Party supporters. This was the second nail in the Brexit Party coffin.

The third was the failure to grasp an opportunity to issue a manifesto that promoted a national vision for the UK, clear objectives for the Transition Period and a full description of how the Party's policies relating to Brexit should be implemented. No other party had proposed such things and The Brexit Party failed to fill the void.

The Brexit Party's resultant poor showing in the the 2019 general election, combined with the short term single issue cause summed up in its name combined to make the Brexit Party one of the most influential to ever exist in British politics, but also perhaps the shortest lived.

So, Brexit undoubtedly triggered a process of change within and amongst political parties. Whether that change will bring greater clarity as to what the political parties stand for - a prerequisite for effective parliamentary democracy -

time will tell, but I expect so. It may even be that the momentum of change produced will provide advocates of proportional representation with an opportunity to progress their cause.

However, for now, it is to Boris Johnson that management of the next great challenge falls: navigating the Transition Period and extracting the United Kingdom from the European Union ,whilst retaining cordial, cooperative relations and avoiding risk to the economies of either party.

The Transition Period, how it is managed and the trajectory on which the UK emerges will be absolutely crucial in terms of our success going into the future.

Attention to detail will be vital.

The jury is still out as to whether Boris Johnson and his Cabinet possess the vision, strategic acumen and leadership to guide the people of the United Kingdom to a successful, confident, optimistic, prosperous and secure future.

Of course I wish the Prime Minister well, but after he has delivered Brexit, will we need someone of slightly different character to take us confidently to the horizon and beyond? Perhaps we will.

And, where is the opposition that the nation so badly needs now that the Labour Party has been decimated and is in such disarray?

I posit that no longer does the UK require an ideological opposition. The Nation instead needs a constructive pro-Brexit opposition that contributes, but is also able to interrogate every decision and action that the government takes throughout the Transition Period and beyond, judging its efficacy against the criteria of placing the country firmly on the post-Brexit trajectory to success.

However, at the moment, no such opposition exists, either in Westminster or outside. Will it perhaps emerge?

None the less, a strong Prime Minister and a pro-Brexit government are in place. The people and businesses of the United Kingdomn are now, finally, able to start orientating themselves towards and planning for the new reality, rather than having to face continued uncertainty. That is a good thing.

ABOUT THE AUTHOR

Henry Bolton OBE was born in Kenya in 1963. He is best known for having been the leader of the UK Independence Party (UKIP) from September 2017 to February 2018.

He is perhaps less well known for his exploits as a soldier, police officer and international diplomat.

He worked for the world's largest international, governmental security organisation, the 57 nation 'Organisation for Security & Cooperation in Europe' (OSCE), as a Human Rights Officer and, later, as Senior Advisor to its Secretary General. He was a United Nations District Administrator, heading local government in Kosovo; Crisis Management Adviser to the Albanian Deputy Prime Minister and regional head of international ceasefire monitoring operations in Skopje, in what is now the Republic of Northern Macedonia. He was also a senior Security & Defence Policy planner working at the heart of the EU's External Action Service in Brussels.

Henry established the International Border Management Staff College in Tajikistan in 2008 and has assisted the governments of 14 countries to design and implement integrated national border management strategies. He has conducted negotiations with numerous governments at ministerial level and, in 2007, negotiated the OSCE's Central Asian Security Strategy amongst all five Central Asian states, the Russian Federation, the European Union and the United Nations.

For two years (2010-2013), he was 'Supported Commander' alongside the United States Marine Corps 'Supporting Commander', responsible for overseeing the coalition's work to establish governance, the rule of law, infrastructure, healthcare and education in Musa Qala District, Northern Helmand, Afghanistan. He was later heard to describe the Taliban as easier to deal with than UKIP's National Executive Committee.

Henry passed out as top overall cadet from the Royal Military Academy, Sandhurst TA Commissioning Course; received a police commendation for outstanding bravery and, in the 2013 New Year's Honours List, was invested as an Officer in the Most Excellent Order of the British Empire (OBE), for services to international security and stabilisation.

Henry is the founder and leader of the 'Our Nation Party of Great Britain and Northern Ireland'. He is also the former leader of the UK Independence Party (UKIP), a party that he now resolutely disassociates himself from because of its blunt, divisive and socially damaging right-wing politics.

He is the founder and CEO of the think tank 'Centre for (post Brexit) Policy' and an International Advisory Board member for the mental healthcare organisation, 'Peaceful-Mind'. In 2019 he received the African Advancement Forum International Award for "Integrity in Public Service".What is missing now is a pro-Brexit opposition, either inside or outside Westminster, that will interrogate and hold the Conservative government to account at every turn throughout the Transition Period

Printed in Great Britain
by Amazon

15465122R00108